DISCRIMINATION

HISPANIC AMERICANS STRUGGLE FOR EQUALITY

DISCRIMINATION

HISPANIC AMERICANS STRUGGLE FOR EQUALITY

by

JEFFRY JENSEN

Rourke Corporation, Inc.
Vero Beach, Florida 32964

Cover design: David Hundley

For information address the publisher, Rourke Corporation, Inc., P.O. Box 3328, Vero Beach, Florida 32964.

∞ The paper used in this book conforms to the American National Standard for Permanence of Paper for Printed Library Materials, Z39.48-1984.

Library of Congress Cataloging-in-Publication Data

Jensen, Jeffry Michael, 1950-

Hispanic Americans struggle for equality / by Jeffry Jensen.

p. cm. — (Discrimination)

Includes bibliographical references and index.

Summary: Identifies discrimination and discusses how Hispanic Americans have struggled for their civil rights.

ISBN 0-86593-180-1 (alk. paper)

1. Hispanic Americans—Civil rights—Juvenile literature. [1. Hispanic Americans—Civil rights. 2. Ethnic relations.] I. Title. II. Series.

E184.S75J46 1992 92-7471

305.868′073—dc20 CIP

AC

PRINTED IN THE UNITED STATES OF AMERICA

CONTENTS

1 What Is Discrimination? 1
2 The Hispanic Experience 8
3 The Mexican Americans 17
4 The Puerto Ricans 31
5 The Cuban Americans 40
6 The Dominican Americans 50
7 The Central Americans 57
8 The South Americans 67
9 Some Who Made a Difference 74

10 Time Line 82
11 Bibliography 86
12 Media Materials 92
13 Resources 94

Index 99

DISCRIMINATION

HISPANIC AMERICANS STRUGGLE FOR EQUALITY

1 What Is Discrimination?

It is the purpose of this first chapter to clarify what discrimination is and describe its many possible forms. Another term that is often associated with discrimination is prejudice. Prejudice can be defined as a negative feeling toward an individual or a group, whereas discrimination manifests itself in a negative action taken against that individual or group. There is a definite link between the feeling or attitude and the action taken, though it is possible for one to exist without the other. For the purpose of this book, how people behave is of primary concern.

When an individual or group is denied the privileges that the majority of a society's citizens take for granted, then it can be said that the individual or group has been discriminated against. Discrimination deprives people of the rights enumerated by Thomas Jefferson in the *Declaration of Independence* (1776): "life, liberty, and the pursuit of happiness." The United States has attempted in word—if not always in deed—to encourage all of its citizens to live life as a free people. The ideal has not been reached, so the struggle to identify and eliminate discrimination proceeds forward.

It may be helpful at this point to amplify how discrimination has been defined by those who have spoken on the issue. The United Nations has stated that "Discrimination includes any conduct based on a distinction made on groups of natural or social categories, which have not relation either to individual capacities or merits, or to the concrete behavior of the individual person." The "natural and social categories" refer to a person's race, ethnic background, religious persuasion, age, gender, sexual persuasion, disability, economic status, or cultural background. When any one of these categories is used to deny a citizen access to a quality education or adequate housing or a good job, then that citizen has become a victim of discrimination. In 1960, behavioral scientist Aaron Antonovsky defined discrimination as "the effective injurious treatment of persons on grounds rationally irrelevant to the situation." Both of these definitions make the point that discrimination restricts capable citizens from succeeding as they wish, merely because of some natural or social category.

A Worldwide Problem

Discrimination has existed since the beginning of recorded history. One of the major reasons why it has been able to continue having an impact in the contemporary world is because of one group's wish to have dominance over other groups. Through discrimination, a dominant group ensures that it will keep to itself all of the rewards to be had of the society. All subordinate groups are looked upon by the dominant group as being threats to its control. The dominant group views discrimination as necessary and proper. A minority or subordinate group may not be allowed to vote, or live in decent housing, pursue an education, or work at anything but menial labor. The list of restrictions could seem endless to those of a minority. In some countries, the treatment of a minority can be extremely harsh. Members of a minority may be harassed or even murdered. The dominant or ruling group will set behavioral boundaries over which a minority dare not cross. The black Africans of South Africa have been brutalized by the white ruling class. The Native Americans were pushed onto reservations so that the European immigrants to the United States could pursue a life on any patch of land that they chose.

Norma Cantu, an attorney for the Mexican-American Legal Defense Fund in San Antonio, Texas; such organizations are needed to combat discrimination. (Bob Daemmrich/ Uniphoto)

In a society where a dominant group can manipulate the economic and social activities of the subordinate groups, a privileged class has been created. Even though it is likely that discrimination will not allow for the efficient utilization of human resources, and probably will keep the dominant group's share of the economic pie smaller, the dominant group perceives that their share is still larger than all subordinate groups', so members of the dominant group see no reason to alter the status quo. A society in general does not benefit when many of its members suffer from discrimination. Unfortunately, fear and self-interest make it hard for the ruling elite to change their ways. Even if discriminatory laws are repealed, custom or tradition may make it hard to alter behavior. When African Americans began moving out of the South in the hope of finding a better life in the big cities of the North, they were shocked to find that the "enlightened" North did not welcome them with open arms.

The whites of the North may have played lip service to the plight of the African Americans who struggled to survive in the South, but when it came to having these same people living in their neighborhoods or attending their churches they found reasons to deny access. Discrimination shows people at their worst. In South Africa, the ruling white community has kept the black Africans from participating fully in the society. They cannot live in white neighborhoods or go swimming on white beaches. Race has been used to separate an entire group. Discrimination has been institutionalized in a country like South Africa. The law of the land is that blacks should lead segregated lives and not share in the prosperity of the white population. It is hoped that through the efforts of brave individuals and pressure from outside forces that the system of apartheid in South Africa will soon come to a just demise.

Hatred of one group for another has led to some unspeakable brutality. Hatred may stem from the stereotyping of a particular group because of a person's isolated negative experience with one member of that particular group. If one member of a minority steals something from a member of the elite, then the individual from the elite may generalize that all members of the minority are thieves. Isolated experiences end up reinforcing negative attitudes that may have already existed. Because of the disease AIDS, many people wish to segregate those who suffer from the disease, so that they cannot infect anyone else. Since many of the victims of this dreaded disease in the United States have been gay, AIDS has reinforced the prejudices of those who believe that gays should not be granted the full privileges of the general society. This example shows how prejudice and discrimination become intertwined.

Unfortunately, history shows that people often feel better about themselves when they are able to subjugate someone else. One person's self-esteem can be enhanced when there is someone weaker to push around. The need for personal security can lead to blatant discrimination. Europeans left their homelands in search of a better life, only to end up brutalizing the native inhabitants of North America. One set of customs came in contact with another set and therefore a struggle ensued. In 1492, 100,000 Jews were forced to leave Spain because they had not converted to Christianity. In this particular case, religion was used to discriminate against the Jews. They have been persecuted for centuries because of their religious ways. At the end of World War II, it was discovered that the Germans had killed six million Jews in concentration camps designed for mass extermination. Known as the Holocaust, this systematic slaughter of Jewish people is one of the most horrendous examples of discrimination in recorded history. Genocide—the attempt to murder an entire group—is the ultimate form of discrimination.

Resistance to Discrimination

While some victims of discrimination are powerless to resist, there have been many protest movements that have attempted to right the wrongs of discrimination. During the 1960's in the United States, thousands of people participated in the Civil Rights movement to fight for racial equality. A number of laws were eventually passed which outlawed discrimination. However, because racial discrimination was so deeply rooted in American society, it has not gone away quietly. There are still plenty of examples of racial discrimination in the United States even though it has been institutionally outlawed. Women throughout the world have had hard lives because they have not been thought of as equal citizens. In certain societies, women are treated as no more than the property of men. Mistreatment of women may not be as prevalent as it was centuries ago, but it was not until the twentieth century that most industrialized countries gave women the vote. Because of economic necessity, there are more women entering the work force. It has been shown that women doing the same work as men are not being paid the same. Some of the activities which contemporary women pursue go against tradition. In this case, tradition speaks in favor of continued gender discrimination.

In the 1980's, a greater awareness of the plight of the disabled came to the fore. Ramps and special handles have become standard equipment for most new buildings. The disabled have been discriminated against because of a physical impairment. They have not been able to go to work like the majority of citizens, because the way the work environment was constructed made it impossible. In ever increasing numbers, the disabled have taken their rightful place in society. They have been denied equal treatment because of their disability, without regard for their talents and what they could contribute to society.

People's age has also been used against them in a number of countries. Industrialized countries have set arbitrary ages at which people must retire from their job. Retirement in and of itself is not necessarily bad, but when the choice to retire has been removed from the individual, then discrimination is involved. It is also true that young people have had restrictions placed on them merely because of their age. Before the Twenty-sixth Amendment to the United States Constitution, a young male could be drafted into the military, but could not vote. With the Twenty-sixth Amendment, the voting age was lowered from twenty-one to eighteen. There seem to be an infinite number of

Eighteen-year-olds in Austin, Texas, vote for the first time; active participation in the democratic process is one of the best strategies against discrimination. (Bob Daemmrich/ Uniphoto)

reasons or excuses for exercising discriminatory practices against someone.

Whatever goes against the grain becomes a threat to the dominant group. In some countries, it has taken a revolution for change to take place. Awareness of what discrimination is and how it works is an important first step to altering the status quo. Laws might be passed, but the changing of how someone feels is an even tougher task. First and foremost, it is behavior patterns that are crucial. That is why the issue of discrimination is so monumental. It may be almost impossible to force someone to like or trust someone else, but it is to the greater good of the general society that no one be hindered from pursuing whatever and wherever their talents will take them. Diversity among peoples is a fact of life, but the pursuit of power has blinded some individuals to the damage that they may be causing their own country. Almost all immigrant groups to a country have found themselves the victims of discrimination at one point or another. Immigrants are vulnerable to the already dominant group. They may even fight amongst themselves in the attempt to move up the social ladder.

As it has been made evident, discrimination is more than merely avoiding someone. It is active and destructive. Coercion, segregation, relocation, even annihilation are all versions of discrimination. Fortunately, strides have been made in the identification and elimination of discriminatory practices. Public protest has helped to heighten awareness of the plight of many minority groups, and in a number of instances, protest has led governments to enact corrective legislation in order to put an end to discriminatory practices. Minority groups have also helped themselves. Pride and a sense of self-worth go a long way to prodding an individual forward against even the heaviest odds.

2 The Hispanic Experience

Hispanic Americans are people of Spanish-speaking descent. There were Hispanics living in the Southwest and Southeast of North America before those regions became part of the United States. Many Hispanics have come to the United States from Mexico, Puerto Rico, Cuba, and the Dominican Republic. Hispanic immigrants have come from El Salvador, Guatemala, and other countries in Central America; some although not as many, have come from countries in South America.

According to figures from the 1990 Census, Hispanics are the second largest minority group in the United States. Blacks, the largest minority group, number about thirty million, followed by Hispanics at 22,354,059. It has been estimated that, because of the large number of Hispanic immigrants and the relatively high Hispanic birthrate, Hispanics will become the largest minority group in the United States by the early years of the twenty-first century.

Hispanic Americans are an extremely diverse group. Many people outside the Hispanic community fail to recognize this diversity. Cuban Americans and Mexican Americans, for example, are different from one another in many ways. They eat different foods, listen to different kinds of music, and speak different varieties of Spanish. Hispanics are racially diverse as well: Whites, blacks, and the native Indian people of Mexico, Central America, South America, and the Caribbean are all represented in the ancestry of today's Hispanic community.

The Roots of Hispanic Culture

With all this diversity, what identifies Hispanics as a group? The answer lies in history. All of the places in which Hispanic culture developed were once part of the far-flung Spanish empire. The Spanish took control of the Americas during the 1500's. In 1565, the Spanish founded St. Augustine, Florida. It was the first permanent European settlement in North America. Florida remained under the control of Spain until 1763 when the English took control. The Spanish regained dominion over Florida in 1783. It was not until 1821 that Florida became a territory of the United States. Spanish explorers were also active in the Southwest during the 1500's. The Spanish called the area New Mexico. They had conquered Mexico in 1521. Mexico did not become an independent country until 1821, and at the time it included the area known as New Mexico. Westward expansion in the United States put pressure on Mexico to give up some of its

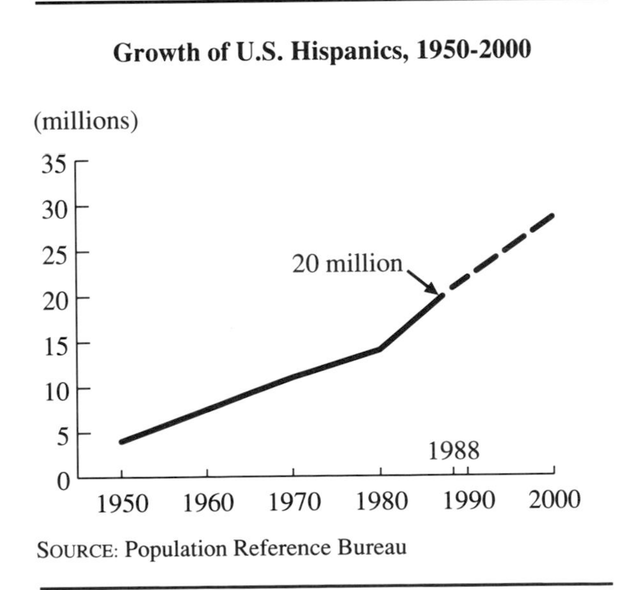

Santa Barbara Mission; the Catholic Church has played a vital role in Hispanic culture. (Susan Hormuth)

territory. After fighting the Mexican War, the United States and Mexico signed the Treaty of Guadalupe Hidalgo in 1848. With the treaty, the United States forced Mexico to accept the annexation of Texas, and took control of a vast amount of territory which includes the present-day states of California, Arizona, Nevada, New Mexico, Utah, and parts of Colorado and Wyoming.

Immigration to the United States

Because of the Mexican Revolution in 1910, large numbers of Mexicans immigrated across the border. Between 1910 and 1930, almost 700,000 Mexicans came to the United States. For the most part, they settled in the Southwest. They took jobs on railroads, ranches, farms, or in mines. They were not welcomed by the local inhabitants. They found it difficult to find decent housing, and they were not paid well for the jobs they did. They found it necessary to organize so as to fight for higher wages. In 1929, the League of United Latin American Citizens (LULAC) was formed. The immigration law of 1917 stated that all adult immigrants were required to read and write at least one language. The United States was trying very hard to discourage Hispanic immigration. In 1924, the Bureau of Immigration found it necessary to establish the Border Patrol. It was the purpose of the patrol to control the number of undocumented workers who were crossing into the United States. During the 1930's, the discrimination against Mexican Americans increased. The depression was hard on everybody, but some people resented the Mexicans who would work at anything they could get, while many people from the dominant group were unemployed. Many Mexicans were forced to return to Mexico under a repatriation program. It was supposed to be a voluntary program, but that was not always the case. Detention camps were set up to house the Mexicans. There even were Mexicans who were citizens of the United States who ended up being deported also. This particular program brought about a good deal of mistrust in the Hispanic community for the true motives of the dominant culture.

Mexican Americans found themselves excluded from public swimming pools and theaters. In the public schools, they were not allowed to speak Spanish. Even with the harsh treatment, there were a large number of Mexican Americans who volunteered for the military after the United States entered World War II. When the war ended, they came home with a sense of accomplishment. They wished to be considered citizens with all the privileges that a white citizen would have. Change was not going to be easy though, and so they formed organizations for the purpose of fighting discrimination. The Mexican American Political Association (MAPA) and the American G.I. Forum were created for this purpose. Between 1942-1947 and 1951-1964, *bracero* (manual laborer) programs were used to make up for the shortage of agricultural and railroad workers. These laborers were allowed to cross the border with the blessing of the U.S. Government. For the most part, they were exploited by harsh employers, but they took the jobs because they needed the work.

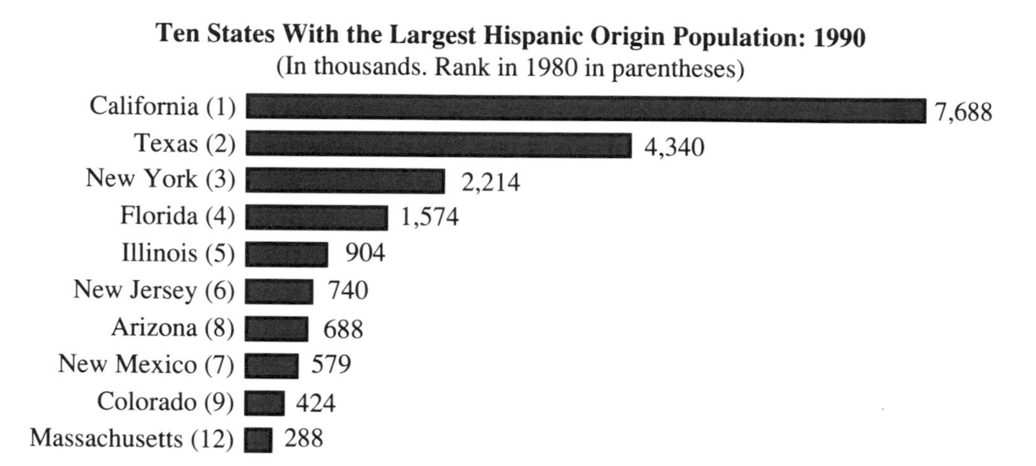

Ten States With the Largest Increases in Hispanic Origin Population: 1980 to 1990

(In thousands)

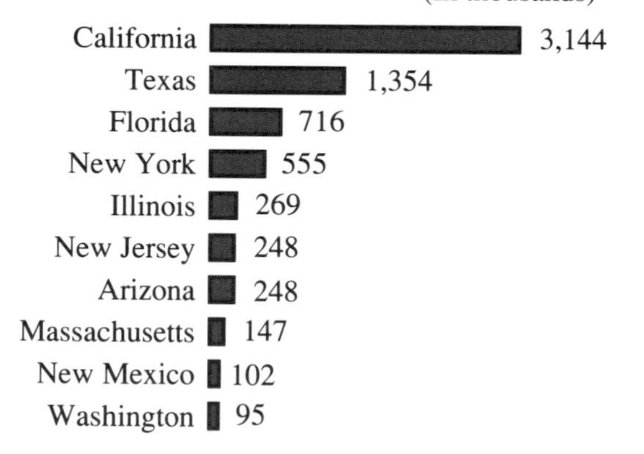

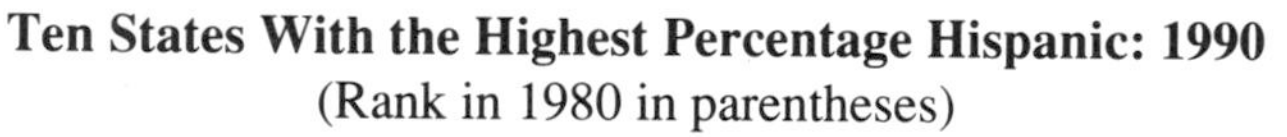

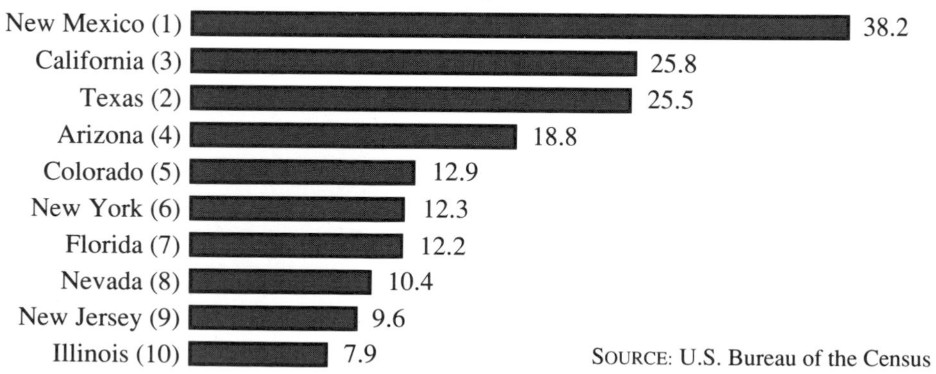

In the 1950's, many Hispanics entered the United States from Mexico, Cuba, and Puerto Rico. Puerto Rico has been a U.S. possession since 1898 and Puerto Ricans became U.S. citizens in 1917. After they became citizens, they could enter the country without restrictions. Looking for a better life, many Puerto Ricans came to New York City. Into the 1990's, New York City still remains the first choice of migration for Puerto Ricans. It has not been easy for them to succeed. Unemployment has remained high since many of the unskilled jobs which they filled no longer exist. They constitute one of New York City's largest minorities. The Puerto Ricans have run into many of the same problems that are common to other Hispanic groups. Language is a barrier and, unless they can receive a good education, the better jobs will remain out of reach for them. Improvements have been made and there are a number of Puerto Rican organizations and associations that were founded to help them. They put on festivals in New York City which have become cultural events for the city as a whole. The most important Puerto Rican cultural organization is the Instituto de Puerto Rico. Even though they come to the United States as citizens, they still face most of the same problems against which other Hispanic groups struggle.

Because of the political turmoil in Cuba during the 1950's, there was a drastic increase in Cuban immigration. In 1959, Fidal Castro violently came to power in Cuba. As a Communist, it was his desire to restructure Cuban society. Many well-to-do Cubans found it necessary to leave the country. By the early 1960's, almost 200,000 Cubans fled Cuba for the United States. The Cubans were welcomed because they were fleeing an oppressive Communist regime. The federal government helped the Cubans find jobs and housing. Because the first refugees were generally well-educated, it was not hard for them to qualify for skilled employment. Cuban immigrants who came after them, were not as well-educated and they were forced to take any job that they could get. In 1980, Castro sent 125,000 Marielitos to the United States. The Marielitos included the unskilled, the mentally ill, and some criminals.

Like this police officer, an increasing number of Hispanic American women are working outside the home. (Bob Daemmrich/Uniphoto)

Miami, Florida has the largest Cuban American population. There is a section of the city which is known as Little Havana. Cuban Americans can also be found in other major U.S. cities. Cuban Americans have not had as difficult a time adjusting to their adopted country as other Hispanic groups. The poverty rate among Cuban Americans is much lower than that for other Hispanics. The United States has become a haven for the majority of those who wished to leave Cuba. Cuban Americans still feel strongly about their native land, and many will be happy when the day arrives that Castro no longer exerts griplike control of Cuba.

Central and South Americans have come to the United States in the attempt to escape oppressive governments and poverty. There are a number of Central American countries that are embroiled in civil wars. Scared for their very survival, Central Americans have come to America. Because the number of refugees is ever increasing, the federal government has attempted to differentiate between those who fled to save their lives and those merely looking for a better life. There are American churches that will give sanctuary to these refugees even though the government believes that they should be sent back to the country of their origin.

Until 1930, Dominicans could enter the Untied States without any problem. When Rafael Trujillo came to power, Dominican immigration was tightly restricted. Trujillo did not allow his subjects to leave the Dominican Republic. After his death in 1961, the flow of immigrations greatly increased. Because of overpopulation, Dominicans did not see much hope of finding work on the island that they share with Haiti. The early Dominican immigrants settled in New York City. In recent years, they have settled in other metropolitan areas of the northeast. A large percentage of Dominicans can be categorized as mulatto. Because of this fact, they have been labeled as black in the United States. This has made for an added burden to their assimilation into American society.

Migrant farm workers. (Bob Daemmrich/Uniphoto)

The Struggle for Equality

By the 1990's, the Hispanic American population had become the fastest growing minority in the United States. Sometime early in the twenty-first century, the Hispanic population will become the largest minority in the country. The Hispanic community does not constitute a monolithic group. There is a great deal of diversity within those who are labeled "Hispanic." Because of their growing numbers, their concerns for better educational opportunities and for higher paying jobs will have to be addressed by United States governmental agencies.

Hispanic Americans have struggled against discrimination ever since they first arrived. In the 1960's, there was a more concerted effort to fight against injustices done to them. Some Hispanics have had better luck in making a good life for themselves in the United States. Education is still a major issue for Hispanic Americans. Bilingual education was mandated by law in 1968. It was hoped that this program would wipe out inadequacies of the educational system, because unless the educational level of Hispanic Americans can be dramatically raised it will continue to be difficult for them to obtain professional jobs. Advocates of bilingual education argue that it serves as a bridge for Hispanic youths to enter the mainstream of American society. The program has remained controversial, and there are those within the Hispanic community who have expressed dismay at the lack of progress bilingual education has made. Illegal immigration is also a sensitive issue, and debate continues both inside and outside the Hispanic community on how best to handle the problem. In the future, creative approaches must be sought to overcome the barriers to equality.

3 The Mexican Americans

The country of Mexico shares a common border with the United States. The border is two thousand miles long and runs from the Pacific Coast of California to Texas. Present-day Mexico consists of more than 750,000 square miles. Historically, the first inhabitants of Mexico were Indians. From about A.D. 500 to 900, the great civilization of the Mayas controlled much of Mexico and Central America. The second spectacular Indian civilization to appear was the Aztecs. They flourished from 1300 until 1519, when Mexico was invaded by Spanish conquistadors. Under the command of Hernán Cortés, five hundred Spanish soldiers destroyed the Aztec empire by 1521 and changed the face of Mexico forever. The Spanish conquerors forced the Indians to work for them as slaves, and Spanish clerics converted them to Roman Catholicism. The Indian population was greatly reduced through brutal treatment and European diseases.

Mexico Under Spanish Control

The land that the Spanish had claimed for themselves became known as "New Spain." The Spanish were interested in exploring areas beyond their current control. In 1540, Francisco Vasquez de Coronado explored northern Mexico in what has become Arizona, New Mexico, Texas, and Kansas. Throughout the

The conquest of Mexico. (Library of Congress)

remaining years of the sixteenth century, Spanish migration pushed to the north. A number of missions were established for the purpose of defense against attacks by North American Indians. Besides Spanish soldiers, there were families and missionaries who moved into the uncharted territory.

In Spanish Mexico, the class system was the same as it was in Spanish Cuba and Puerto Rico. The ruling class was made up of whites who had been born in Spain. This ruling class was called *gachupines*. The aristocrats of the colonial society were the whites who had been born in Mexico, called *criollos* or Creoles. These white groups brutalized the Indian population and denied them many rights including schooling, decent jobs, and personal liberties. Because there was a shortage of eligible women, intermarriage between Creole men and Indian women was not uncommon; through this intermarriage a new class was created known as Mestizos. It was also possible that a Mestizo could have African blood, since the Spanish had brought thousands of

MEXICO

black Africans to Mexico for slave labor. Within this colonial society, the standard of living remained fairly low, except for the ruling elite. The Indians were exploited for the benefit of the Spanish empire, and the Catholic Church did very little to make the daily lives of the Indians better.

By the end of the eighteenth century, Spanish settlements had been established throughout California, Arizona, New Mexico, and Texas. Mestizos and Mexican Indians made up the majority of the settlers. Life in these settlements was hard; for both of these groups, chances for advancement made them endure all the hardships. In the frontier territory, the mestizos could become soldiers or low-level officials. Some of the important settlements were Los Angeles and San Diego in California, Tucson in Arizona, Santa Fe in New Mexico, and Laredo, San Antonio, and El Paso in Texas. There was a great deal of frustration among the citizens of New Spain over how Spain controlled their colony. There was even talk that maybe Spain should no longer control them at all. The American and French Revolutions sparked thoughts of independence among the New Spaniards. After Napoleon's French forces invaded Spain in 1808 and eventually defeated Spain, Napoleon installed his brother Joseph on the Spanish throne. The people of New Spain realized that the Spanish crown could no longer exert control over them.

Independent Mexico

In 1821, Mexico finally won its independence from Spain. The northern territories were ignored for the most part by the independence-minded activists in Mexico City. Trappers and merchants from the United States had begun moving into the northern Mexican territories. The migration in some areas was so great that the Americans became powerful there. Open hostilities broke out in these areas between the Mexicans and the Americans. The newly created Republic of Mexico did very little to better the lot of the poor. One military leader after another

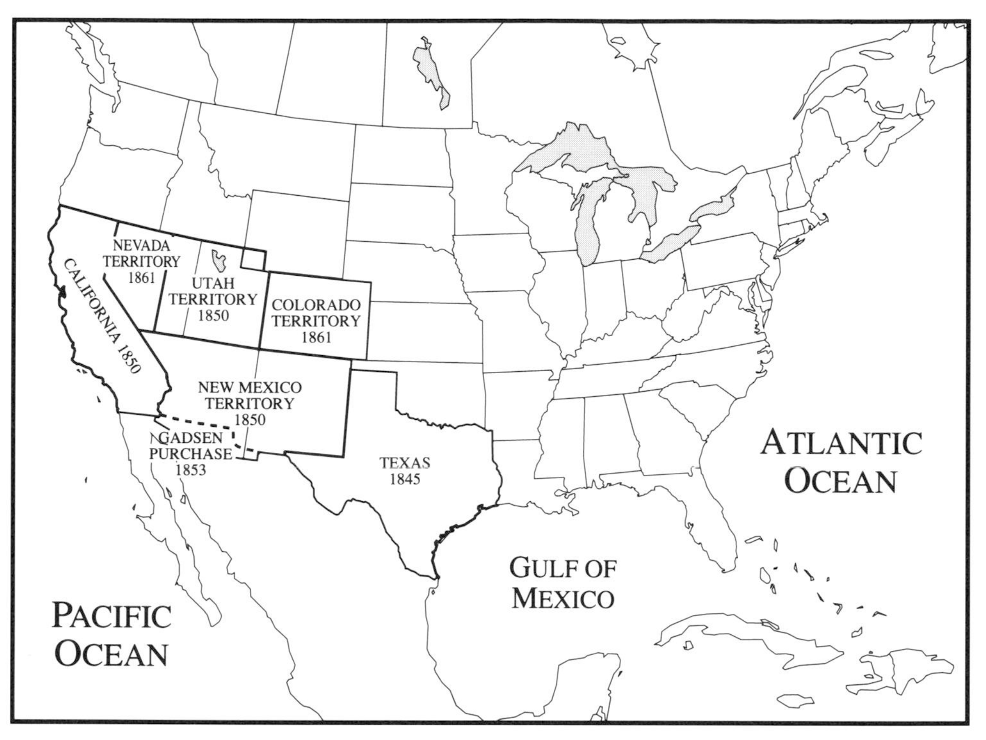

States and Territories Formed from Territory That Once Was Mexico

took control of Mexico, and focused more on keeping control than on benefiting the general population. In the 1820's, the Mexican government encouraged Anglo-Americans to settle on the prairies of Texas. A conflict erupted soon after when the Americans wished to transport slavery into the territory. Mexican authorities did not approve of slavery being introduced into Texas. By the 1830's, approximately thirty thousand Americans were living in Texas. The inhabitants of Texas—which included Anglo-Americans and Mexican-Texans—revolted against Mexico in 1836. During the Texan Revolution, the famous Battle of the Alamo was fought in San Antonio. Mexico won this particular battle, but they lost the war and control of Texas.

The First Mexican Americans

The United States annexed Texas in 1845 as a slave state. The Mexicans who stayed in Texas became the first large Mexican group in the United States. The Mexican government refused to recognize the loss of Texas, and also was disturbed by American settlers revolting in California. In 1846, President James Polk declared war on Mexico, and American troops invaded Mexico. Mexican troops were defeated in California, Arizona, and New Mexico. The United States fought the Mexican War in order to expand slave territory. A peace treaty was signed in 1848; Mexico was forced to acknowledge the annexation by the United States of Texas as well as give up California, Arizona, Nevada, New Mexico, Utah, and portions of Colorado and Wyoming. With the Treaty of Guadalupe Hidalgo, the United States agreed to pay Mexico fifteen million dollars, plus three million dollars in war damages. Eighty thousand Mexicans became residents of the United States with this treaty. The treaty allowed them to stay and become American citizens, or they could return to Mexico. The majority of them decided to remain and the Mexicans constituted the majority in California, New Mexico, and Arizona until the discovery of gold in 1849 in northern California. With the completion of the transcontinental railroad in the 1870's, Anglo-Americans came to Arizona in large numbers. By the end of the nineteenth century, the English-speaking population had become the majority in the Southwest.

Within the territory taken by the United States, Mexican Americans became outcasts. They were considered to be inferior by the Anglo population. The United States government made it almost impossible for them to retain the land that had been theirs from before the Mexican War. They would have to go to court to prove that they possessed Spanish land grants. The process could take many years and was very expensive. Anglo-Americans definitely had the upper hand and would resort to devious—even violent—means to take the Mexican Americans' land away from them. By 1900, Mexican Americans found themselves no more than hired hands for the Anglos.

With their dark skin, their Spanish language, and their Catholic religion, Mexican Americans were looked upon as an impediment to Anglo conquest of the Southwest. The Anglos had

Cinco de Mayo, the popular holiday celebrating Mexico's victory over occupying French forces on May 5, 1862. (David Young-Wolff/PhotoEdit)

learned how to be cowboys from the Mexican *vaqueros*. The Mexicans had even developed sheepherding before the Anglos arrived. The Southwestern economies grew rapidly after Anglo-Americans were in control. A number of minorities were used as cheap labor — including African, Mexican, Chinese, and Native Americans — in order to line the pockets of the Anglo population. Even though conditions were harsh for the Southwest Mexicans, the poverty and instability in Mexico made the Southwest look more attractive. The Mexican American population grew from 75,000 in 1890 to 562,000 in 1900. The new immigrants were — for the most part — poor and illiterate.

Border Crossings

The twentieth century brought a massive migration of people from Mexico. Between 1900 and 1940, it is estimated that 750,000 Mexicans crossed the border into the United States. The Mexican economy was not very healthy, especially after 1910 when civil war broke out in Mexico. During this same period, the U.S. economy was booming. The immigrants found employment in factories and mines, and on farms and the railroad. There was no quota on the number of Mexicans who could enter the United States. American employers needed cheap labor, and the Mexicans were eager to work. At the time of World War I, U.S. agricultural and manufacturing production had to be increased, so work restrictions on Mexican Americans were relaxed. They were able to move into skilled positions, such as machinists and mechanics. Some Mexican Americans moved to Chicago and Detroit to find manufacturing jobs. By 1929, the Mexican-born population in the United States had bulged to one million.

The stock market crash of 1929 changed everything for the new immigrants. They were forced out of their jobs in favor of unemployed Anglos. Both state and local governments instituted abusive programs, in the hope of rounding up illegal aliens and sending them back to Mexico. The Mexican Americans who lost their jobs were forced to seek government aid. The Great Depression was hard on everybody, but minorities seemed to be hardest hit by discriminatory practices. There was even a repatriation program instituted with the cooperation of the Mexican government. Under this program, approximately 500,000 individuals of Mexican descent decided to return to Mexico.

Violence Against Mexican Americans

A labor shortage did not appear again until World War II. Mexico and the United States agreed that Mexico would provide *braceros* (manual laborers) with temporary visas; thousands of Mexicans entered the United States. The *bracero* program officially operated between 1942 and 1947, continuing on an unofficial basis between 1951 and 1964. Five million immigrants entered the United States as seasonal workers under the program. Unfortunately, there were Mexican Americans who lost their jobs to the *braceros*. The *braceros* worked for little money and were housed in substandard structures. Because the Mexican immigrants tended to be uneducated and poor, many Anglo-Americans made the generalization that all Mexicans were stupid and lazy.

Anglo stereotyping of Mexican Americans was prevalent in many sections of the Southwest. Mexican Americans were subject to daily prejudice, but on occasion it would erupt into violent episodes. For example, in 1942, police in Los Angeles, California, used the death of José Díaz as an excuse to arrest hundreds of Mexican American youths. The body of Díaz was found in the Sleepy Lagoon. Twenty-two Mexican American youths were placed on trial for the murder of Díaz. Seventeen of these youths were convicted on a variety of charges. In 1943, the Sleepy Lagoon Defense Committee raised money to help appeal the court's decision. A higher court did reverse the lower court's decision. The reversal of the court's decision outraged the Anglo

The Day of the Dead, a festival that reveals the unique fusion of Spanish and Indian elements in Mexican culture. (Felicia Martinez/PhotoEdit)

community and led to the notorious Zoot Suit Riots. (Zoot suitswere a style of clothing popular among Mexican American males at that time.) U.S. servicemen started beating up any Mexican American youth that they could catch. Since the police were prejudiced and refused to protect them, many Mexican American youths began forming gangs in order to protect themselves.

The Culture of the Barrio

Historically, the vast majority of Mexican immigrants have settled in the Southwest, especially California and Texas. As other immigrant groups had done, they tended to find strength in settling together. They moved into *barrios* (neighborhoods) in the poorest sections of town. Discrimination and the security of being together kept them in poverty. East Los Angeles is one of the oldest barrios in the United States. Within the barrio, the Mexican American community attempted to preserve their own traditions and language. Life was made somewhat easier when families could band together. Unfortunately, this separation made it difficult to improve their lot in America. They were forced to attend segregated public schools if they could not afford to attend Catholic parochial schools. It was even tougher for the Mexican migrant workers who had to move from one place to another to work in the fields. The children of migrant parents had to move from school to school, which made it very near impossible to receive a decent education.

With the outbreak of World War II, Mexican Americans proudly joined in the fight against Germany and Japan. Hundreds of thousands of Mexican Americans served in the U.S. military during World War II. After the war, many of them took advantage of the G.I. Bill of Rights, which provided money for veterans to attend college or buy a home. Mexican American veterans formed the G.I. Forum in order to protect their rights.

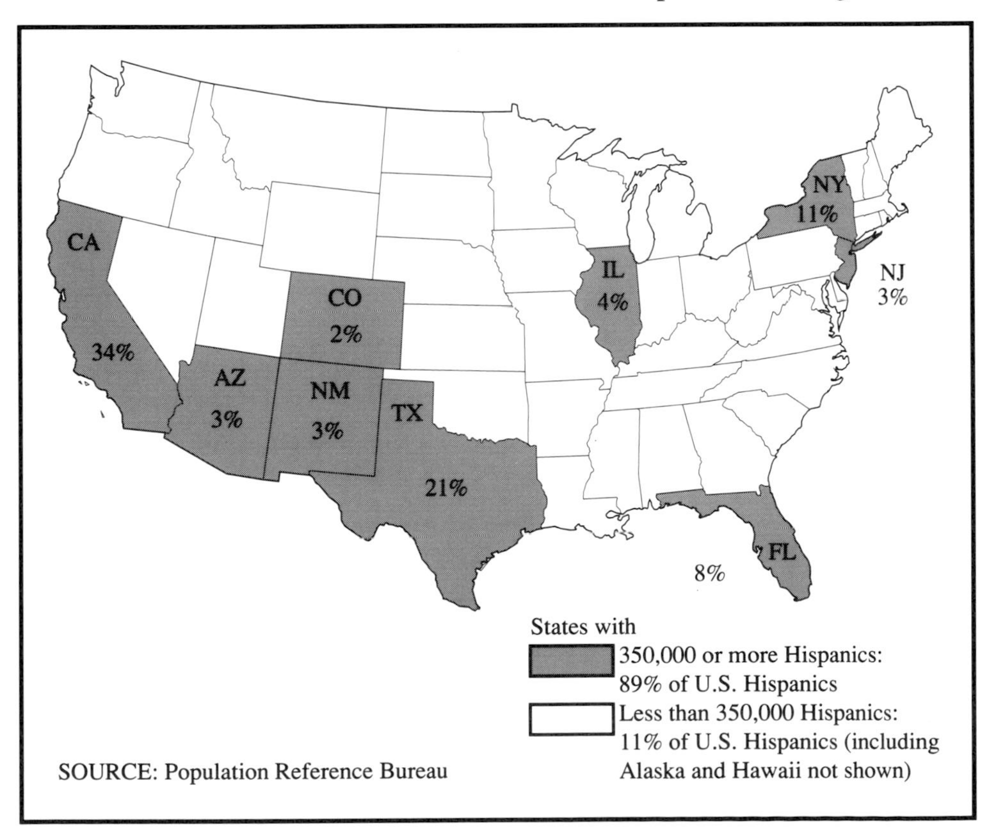

Distribution of U.S. Hispanics by State, 1988

During the 1950's, the United States government became especially concerned about the large number of undocumented Mexicans who were entering the country illegally. Because of the two-thousand-mile border, the U.S. Immigration and Naturalization Service (INS) had an almost impossible task. In 1955, the INS began "Operation Wetback" ("Wetback" being an insulting term referring to the immigrants who crossed the Rio Grande to enter the United States) to round up illegal Mexican immigrants. INS agents would arrest anyone who could not prove their legal status.

The Chicano Movement

When people take pride in themselves and in their culture, they are able to fulfill their potential. In the 1950's, activists such as Reies López Tijerina began to fight prejudice and discrimination by proudly defining themselves as "Chicanos." The term "Chicano" was originally a negative label applied to recent immigrants from Mexico. Tijerina and his fellow activists took this term and began using it in a positive way, to show their pride in their Hispanic cultural heritage and their defiance of prejudice.

In the 1960's, the Chicano movement became powerful, especially among Mexican American students. Just as African American students were demanding courses and programs in Black Studies or African American Studies, so Chicano Studies programs were born. These programs allowed Mexican American students to study their history and encouraged scholars to explore the Mexican American experience, often ignored by mainstream historians. Chicano arts programs and many community services were also established.

Mexican American activists were particularly successful in winning rights for farm workers, who had long been underpaid and mistreated. The long battle against this form of discrimination was led by César Chávez, who organized the farm

Illegal immigration continues to be a controversial issue. (U.S. Immigration Service)

workers into a union. (For a fuller account of Chávez and the migrant workers' struggle, see chapter 9).

Not all Mexican Americans accepted the term "Chicano." Many preferred to identify themselves in other ways. Many were critical of some of the goals and tactics of Chicano leaders. Today, while it is still very much in use, the term "Chicano" is not as widely used in the Mexican American community as it was in the 1960's. (To distinguish the contributions of women, the term "Chicana" is now common.) The legacy of the Chicano movement, however, remains strong.

Bilingual Education

Language had been a major barrier for Mexican Americans to get ahead in the United States. In 1968, President Lyndon B. Johnson signed the Bilingual Education Act. The law directed school districts to establish bilingual education programs. Immigrant students were to be taught in their own language, and there were to be special classes set up to teach them English. It has been a controversial program, and it still is to be determined whether it is the proper way to educate those for whom Spanish is their first language. Mexican Americans represent the largest Hispanic minority in the United States. As of March, 1991, the Census states that they represent 62.6 percent of the 22 million Hispanics. The Chicano movement and school desegregation have given the Mexican American community a new sense of pride. The League of United Latin American Citizens (LULAC)—which was formed in Texas in 1929—fought in the 1960's to desegregate Mexican American schools. The Mexican American Legal Defense and Education Fund (MALDEF) was founded in 1968 for the purpose of protecting the legal rights of Mexican Americans. As of 1988, 54 percent of the Mexican Americans between the ages of twenty-five and thirty-four had completed high school. The yearly median income for a Mexican American family was reported to be $23,200 by the U.S. Census in March, 1991. This median income is $13,000 lower than it is for non-Hispanic families.

These statistics are somewhat misleading because they do not take into account the ever-growing Mexican American middle class, which has established itself over the last few decades. Because there are so many new arrivals who have not found their place in the society and, therefore, have not been able to qualify for skilled jobs, the success of Mexican Americans who have been living in the United States for generations is frequently overlooked.

The cultural celebrations of the Mexican Americans have become part of the United States. Mexican cuisine is very popular, and Tex-Mex music has millions of listeners. Great strides have been made through the efforts of Mexican American activists and others concerned with making life for all Mexican Americans better. The United States will be a truly rich country when all of its citizens can share equally in the same opportunities to prosper.

4 The Puerto Ricans

Puerto Rico is an island that is located about one thousand miles southeast of Florida. It is part of an island chain known as the West Indies. Puerto Rico, Cuba, Jamaica, and Hispaniola (the island divided between Haiti and the Dominican Republic) constitute one part of the chain known as the Greater Antilles. Puerto Rico is the smallest island of the group, with a length of about one hundred miles and a width of thirty-five miles. Because of its green interior and its sandy beaches, Puerto Rico is considered one of the most strikingly beautiful West Indian islands. The Arawak Indians first came to Puerto Rico from South America about two thousand years ago. They were the first inhabitants of the island, which they named "Boriquén" or "Land of the Valiant One." They made a good life for themselves on the island. They were not a warring people, but they learned to defend themselves against a fierce tribe known as the Caribs who attacked Boriquén on many occasions.

Colonial Puerto Rico

On his second voyage to the New World, Christopher Columbus reached Boriquén on November 19, 1493. He was impressed by what he saw and henceforth claimed the island for Spain. Columbus gave the island the new name of San Juan Bautista. Columbus remained on the island for three days; then he and his fleet sailed on to Hispaniola. The Spanish did not send anyone else to the island until 1508, when Ponce de Léon and his men were sent to colonize Boriquén. The island was turned into a military fortress with the hope that it would serve to protect the sea route to Spain's many other colonies. The Indians of the island were forced into slavery by the Spanish conquerors. The Arawaks had to work in the gold mines and on the farms that were under the control of the Spanish. The Indians became so frustrated with their enslavement that they rebelled against their European masters. Spanish soldiers were ordered to shoot the Arawaks who refused to work. The majority of the tribe were either killed or died from European diseases which had been brought to the island. The Spanish decided that the Indians were no longer dependable as laborers, so in 1511 the first black African slaves were imported to the island. The slaves would be used as forced laborers until slavery was outlawed in 1873. The

WEST INDIES

island would remain a Spanish possession until 1898. During Spain's centuries of control, the inhabitants of Puerto Rico became a mixture of Spanish, African, and Native American.

Puerto Ricans rebelled against the Spanish colonizers a number of times during the nineteenth century. They began migrating to the United States as political exiles who needed refuge in order to plot independence movements. Puerto Rico and Cuba were the only remnants of Spain's empire in the New World by the mid-nineteenth century. The United States was more than casually interested in both the islands. There were American businesses which controlled economic interests in Puerto Rico and Cuba, such as the owning of a number of sugar plantations. With the sinking of the American battleship *Maine* in 1898, the United States declared war with Spain. The Spanish-American War lasted a mere ten weeks; when it was over, the United States had defeated Spain and taken control of the Philippines, Puerto Rico, and Cuba. On December 10, 1898, Spain signed the Treaty of Paris, and Puerto Rico became an American possession.

American Control

Whereas Puerto Ricans had hoped that they would eventually win their independence from Spain, the results of the Spanish-American War merely meant that they were now under the control of the United States. After 1898, the Puerto Rican poor began emigrating to New York City. In 1900 with the Foraker Act, Puerto Rico was granted a certain degree of self-government. Puerto Ricans were still not happy with their situation. In 1917, the United States Congress passed the Jones Act, which made Puerto Ricans citizens of the United States. The pressure for independence had brought the Puerto Ricans citizenship to the country that controlled their lives. The Jones Act was widely resented by Puerto Ricans. Because of the act, Puerto Rico became an "organized but unincorporated" territory of the United States. Under this new arrangement, Puerto Rico's economy expanded. Sugar production was a major factor in this expansion. During the first twenty-five years of the twentieth century, Puerto Rico's population increased by more than a million people. With this increase in population, Puerto Rico became one of the most densely populated areas in the world. Even though the economy had improved, most of the profits derived from sugar, tobacco, and tourism found its way into the pockets of the large American investors. The common workers of Puerto Rico saw little improvement in their daily lives. Life was hard for the majority of Puerto Ricans and a number of them looked at moving to the United States as a way out of poverty.

Immigration to the United States

In 1910, there were no more than 1,500 Puerto Ricans living in the United States. In the next ten years, the number of Puerto Ricans living in New York alone increased to 7,000. Since air travel would not be introduced until the 1940's, the Puerto Ricans had to transport themselves to the mainland by boat. The United States passed restrictive laws in 1921 and 1924, but since Puerto Ricans were citizens, the laws did not affect them. New York City was the city of choice for the majority of Puerto Ricans. Of the more than 53,000 Puerto Ricans who lived in America by 1930, more than 45,000 of them had settled in New York City. They found employment in factories, the garment industry, hospitals, laundries. It was not easy for the Puerto Ricans to adjust to life in the United States. Spanish was the language of Puerto Rico, and most of those who came to the mainland could not speak English. The cold climate of New York in the winter was something that was totally foreign to the Puerto Ricans; the Caribbean weather of the island was generally warm throughout all year round. Because of the dire economic conditions in Puerto Rico during the Depression years of the 1930's, the United States looked to be a better place to find a job.

Between 1940 and 1950, the total Puerto Rican population in the United States increased from 70,000 to 300,000, and the total

Spanish-language magazines are in demand for the vibrant and steadily growing Hispanic community. (Bill Aron/PhotoEdit)

number living in New York City bulged to 187,000. When it became possible for them to fly from Puerto Rico to America in merely a few hours, the migration of Puerto Ricans was dramatically increased. Even though the United States looked to be the land of opportunity, Puerto Ricans found a foreign culture that discriminated against them. Color and language made them the target for prejudicial treatment. For the most part, the only jobs that Puerto Ricans could get were either unskilled or semiskilled positions. Upon arriving in the United States, they found that color affected where they could live and what kind of job they could get. Many of the Puerto Rican women took jobs in the garment industry, where the wages were low and the working conditions were unsafe. The majority of migrants who came to New York City after World War II found it necessary to settle in rundown areas of the city which had been vacated by previous immigrant groups. A large Puerto Rican community had taken root in East Harlem and became known as "El Barrio." In the postwar years, they moved into the South Bronx as well as Manhattan's Lower East and Upper West Side. Limited educational opportunities and the language barrier made it very difficult for the Puerto Ricans to work in anything but menial jobs as well as move out of the crumbling neighborhoods of New York City.

Because of the overcrowded conditions in New York, some Puerto Ricans came to the conclusion that they should move to other cities such as Chicago and Boston. Prejudice was no less evident in the other cities to which the Puerto Ricans moved. Parents were willing to endure hardships as long as their children could receive a good education in the American schools. Unfortunately, Puerto Rican children faced severe discrimination in the public schools. Since they could not speak or understand English, teachers often labeled them as slow learners. Because of the humiliation, many Puerto Rican children dropped out of school. Some of the youth formed gangs and created a sense of solidarity. By 1980, there were two million Puerto Ricans living on the mainland, and of that two million there were 816,000 making their home in New York City. Even though Puerto Ricans were coming to the mainland to seek a better life, many still felt close to Puerto Rico and had thoughts of returning to the island after they had made enough money to improve their family's economic situation. To have one foot in their country of birth and the other foot in their adopted country, made it difficult for the Puerto Ricans to fully become involved with the political and cultural life of the United States.

Commonwealth Status

In 1949, Puerto Rico elected its own governor for the first time. The new governor, Luis Muñoz Marín, became the first Puerto Rican to govern Puerto Rico. During the first year of his administration, Muñoz established the office of the Commonwealth of Puerto Rico, Department of Labor, Migration Division in order to provide help for those Puerto Ricans who wished to settle in the United States. (Under their commonwealth status, Puerto Ricans retained most of their rights as U.S. citizens. While giving up some benefits, they were not subject to federal income tax.) It was located in New York, and it was established for the purpose of making the transition less traumatic. This was very unusual for a government to follow its citizens into their adopted country. Community organizations were slow to get started, but the Puerto Ricans did put their stamp on any section of the city in which they settled. El Barrio was the most famous Puerto Rican community. The businesses of El Barrio had a distinctly Puerto Rican flavor. The theaters would show Spanish-language movies, and stores that had jukeboxes played Spanish records. They would celebrate their heritage with colorful parades. Life was hard, but they refused to give up their cultural roots. During the 1960's, there were some Puerto Ricans who gave up the struggle in the United States and moved back to their island home. Those who stayed came to the realization that if their situation was to improve, then they had to become more

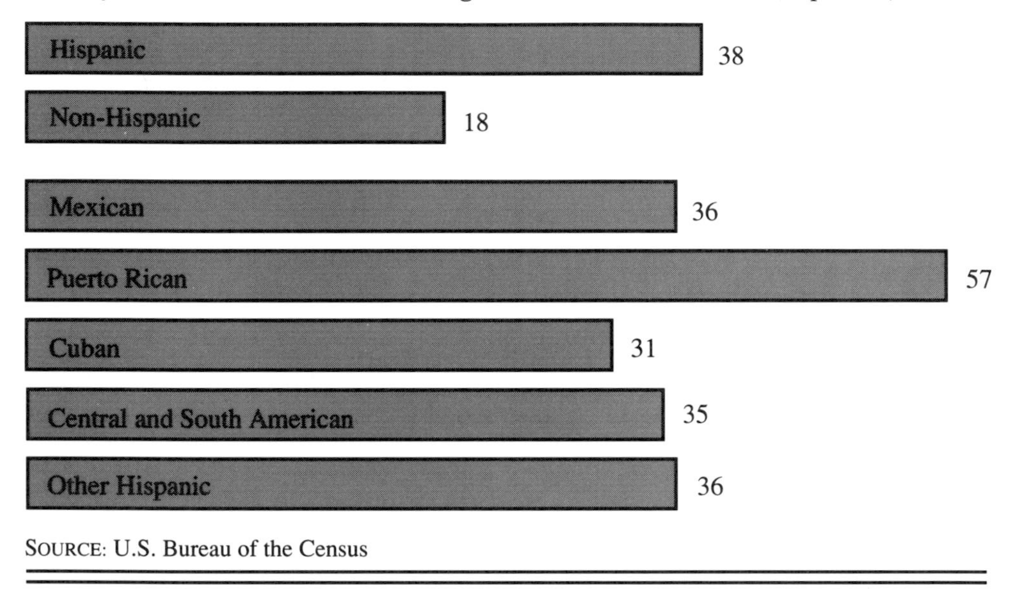

active in the public life of their new country. During the 1970's, Puerto Ricans began to be elected to public office. There had been some important organizations established after World War II.

The Congress of Organizations and Puerto Rican Hometowns was formed in 1958. This association of civic, political, and cultural groups in New York City attempted—among other things—to serve as a bridge between state and city officials and its membership. In the early 1960's, Puerto Ricans formed the National Association for Puerto Rican Civil Rights and the National Puerto Rican-Hispanic Voter Participation Project. Puerto Rican professionals founded the Association of Puerto Rican Executive Directors (ASPIRA) in New York City. These professionals believed that education was the only way for Puerto Rican youth to make it in the United States. Scholarship programs were set up, as well as youth clubs. In 1980, ASPIRA of America was founded and helped to coordinate the efforts of groups that existed in New York, New Jersey, Florida, Illinois, Pennsylvania, and Puerto Rico. They also became crucial in linking groups with government agencies. The largest and oldest nonprofit Puerto Rican community-based organization in the United States, the National Puerto Rican Forum, was founded in

1957. This organization has worked for economic and social improvement of Puerto Ricans and other Hispanics. Because of the forum, the Puerto Ricans living in New York City, have been able to band together with a common purpose of struggling for a better life. Through these—and a number of other concerned organizations—Puerto Ricans have been able to make steady progress in their common pursuit of becoming more in control of their destiny as a people.

Poverty in the Puerto Rican Community

Puerto Ricans are the second largest Hispanic population in the United States. As of March, 1991, the Puerto Rican population constituted an estimated 11.1 percent of the total Hispanic population. The majority of Puerto Ricans have settled in New York, New Jersey, and Chicago. Of all the Hispanic groups, Puerto Ricans are the poorest. The median yearly family income according to the Census for Puerto Ricans is $14,500. In 1990, 37 percent of Puerto Rican families were in poverty, which is higher than any other Hispanic group. One of the most tragic statistics is that as of March, 1990, 57 percent of Puerto Rican children live in poverty.

Puerto Ricans have had a very tough time trying to make their way in the United States. There is a lot of work that needs to be done in the future if they are to succeed. Education will have to play a major role as many Puerto Ricans have already surmised. As of 1988, 67 percent of Puerto Ricans between the age of twenty-five and thirty-four had completed high school. The passage of the Bilingual Education Act of 1968 and the implementation of bilingual programs in the schools has to some degree helped Puerto Ricans to receive a better education. Bilingual education is a controversial issue in many areas of the country and some school systems have had to have legal action brought against them so that bilingual programs could be initiated. But there are Puerto Rican children who have benefited from bilingual education.

5 The Cuban Americans

Like Puerto Rico, Cuba is part of the Greater Antilles chain of islands. It is the largest island of the chain, measuring 777 miles in length and between nineteen and 119 miles in width. Cuba is a mere ninety miles away from Florida. The island has been called the "pearl of the Antilles." In 1492, Christopher Columbus became the first European to land on Cuba. The Arawak Indians already inhabited the island. A peaceful people, they were no match for the Spanish. In 1511, Diego Velázquez colonized Cuba and within six years the Indians on the island had virtually been wiped out by mistreatment, disease, and even suicide. The Spanish were forced to import black African slaves to work the sugar plantations. Cuban society was changed forever with the introduction of African slaves. The number of Africans added to the island increased to a point that by 1800, they greatly outnumbered the white colonists. Sugar and tobacco were the leading exports of Cuba, and by the mid-nineteenth century Cuba had become the world's largest exporter of sugar.

American Interest in Cuba

The United States' interest in Cuba can be traced back to Thomas Jefferson. In 1848, President James Polk went so far as to offer Spain one hundred million dollars for the purchase of

Cuba, but the Spanish were not impressed by the amount; in fact, they were outraged. The United States did not lose interest in the island. It merely had to wait for the opportune moment when they could annex Cuba. Cuban immigrants had been living in Florida as far back as the 1830's. A Cuban cigar factory had been started in Key West, Florida. A number of tobacco workers came to the United States after 1868 because of the Cuban independence movements that would attack tobacco plantations to further their cause. The most famous Cuban revolutionary of the late nineteenth century, José Martí, spent time as an exile in the United States. Cigar makers who had already relocated in Tampa, Key West, and New York supported Martí's revolutionary aspirations.

The period between 1868 and 1878 was one of turmoil in Cuba. An armed conflict known as the Ten Years' War cost the lives of 250,000 Cubans. The Cuban separatists were badly defeated. The United States accepted the separatists who fled as refugees. The number of refugees bulged to five thousand after the war. José Martí lived in the United States from 1880 until 1895, when he returned to Cuba to fight for its independence. Martí was killed by the Spanish forces on May 19, 1895 at the Battle of Dos Ríos. In 1898, the American battleship *Maine* was blown up while it was in Havana's harbor. The United States had been looking for a legitimate excuse to remove Spain from its remaining colonial holdings in the hemisphere and the sinking of the *Maine* led to the United States declaring war on Spain. In little more than two months, the Spanish-American War was over and the United States found itself in control of Cuba, Puerto Rico, and the Philippines. American troops occupied Cuba from 1898 until 1902.

Cubans had hoped that they could now consider themselves free and independent of all colonial powers, but the United States was not about to give up all influence over the island so soon after they had liberated it from the Spanish. The United States got Cuba to agree to the Platt Amendment in 1901, which allowed for an American naval base to be built on Guantánamo

Bay and the right for the United States to interfere in Cuban affairs when it was deemed in Cuba's best interest. Cuba became a republic in 1902, but for all practical purposes, Cuba was an American colony. Americans invested heavily in Cuban sugar production. Unfortunately, the Cuban workers remained poor as American corporations reaped large profits. Besides sugar, American investors found it profitable to put large funds in Cuban agriculture, banking, and transportation.

The Batista Regime

The Cuban republic was run by a succession of corrupt governments. Fulgencio Batista took control of Cuba in 1933 with the secret support of the United States. His rule of Cuba lasted from 1933 until he was overthrown by Fidel Castro in 1959. During the Batista era, Havana became like a playground for rich Americans looking for a good time. In the early years of his rule, Batista built schools, improved health care, and legalized labor unions, but he became more like a dictator as time went on and there was dissatisfaction with his undemocratic measures. During the last few years of his dictatorship, as many as 15,000 Cubans migrated to the United States. Any Cuban who felt that he had fallen out of favor or had lost his job knew that it was in his own best interest to seek refuge in America.

Fidel Castro and the Cuban Exodus

In 1959, Castro and his rebel forces ousted Batista and many of Batista's supporters fled to the United States. A massive migration did not begin until after Castro announced that he was going to alter Cuban society completely. The United States government was displeased with the course of events. Former Cuban officials and military personnel had to leave Cuba in order to avoid imprisonment or even death. After Castro declared

A Cuban American architect in Miami; many of the Cubans who came to the U.S. after Castro took power were affluent, well-educated professionals. (Library of Congress)

Bilingual signs such as this are common in Miami's Cuban community. (Library of Congress)

himself to be a Marxist-Leninist and said that the Communist Party would dictate how the country was to be organized, many landowners and industrialists recognized that it was time to leave Cuba. Between 1959 and 1962, more than 155,000 Cubans left their homeland for the United States. Because they were fleeing what was perceived as a sinister Communist government, the Cuban immigrants were granted refugee status by the United States government. The majority of the Cubans who came in this wave of immigrants were well-educated. Diplomatic relations between Cuba and the United States became so shaky that the Eisenhower Administration decided to sever relations completely on January 3, 1961.

Cubans agonized about leaving their beloved country, but with their whole way of life being disrupted by Communist ideology, they made the tough decision and left for America. They believed, though, that they would be returning to Cuba once

Castro was overthrown. The exiles—as a whole—were from the upper or upper-middle classes of Cuban society. 31 percent of the refugees were either professional, technical, or managerial workers. The majority settled only 150 miles away from Cuba in Miami, Florida. Miami had already been established as the destination of choice for Cubans, since the climate and environment reminded them of their native Cuba. There were already 46,000 Cubans living in Miami when this massive wave of immigrants began arriving. The United States government was not prepared to handle such a large number of refugees. It has been estimated that approximately 1,600 of them came to Miami each week between 1960 and 1965. The Cuban Refugee Emergency Center in Miami was established in 1960 by the United States government. The center came to the aid of 77 percent of the Cubans who arrived from 1960 to 1963. The majority of Cubans helped by the center settled in the Miami area, but the center also started a relocation program so that the city would not become overburdened. Through the center, the refugees received food, health services, financial aid, plus free vocational training and instruction in English.

Little Havana

Miami was fast becoming like a second Havana. A section of the city even became known as "Little Havana." The Cubans were very industrious people and many rundown sections of Miami were given a facelift through hard work and special low-interest loans from the U.S. government. A definite Cuban flavor was now part of the mix that was Miami. They established restaurants, retail businesses, and night clubs. There were other Cuban communities that sprang up in many states, including New York, New Jersey, California, and Illinois. Life was frustrating for many middle-class Cubans since they could not step into the same employment situation on the mainland that they had in Cuba. They had to take whatever job they could get and work themselves back up to a comparable position. The elderly and the children were the hardest hit by being uprooted from Cuba. Fifteen thousand children had been sent to America by their parents immediately after the revolution in order to save them from becoming pawns in the new Cuba. Once they arrived, it was necessary for them to go to foster homes or orphanages, until either their parents could make the trip to America or a relative could take custody of them.

The Cuban exiles—even though they had begun to make a new start in America—had not given up hope of returning triumphantly to a Cuba liberated from Castro's Communist stranglehold. In 1961, the Bay of Pigs invasion was a complete disaster. There was even some resentment of some Cubans toward the U.S. government, for not doing more to guarantee the success of the attempted retaking of Cuba. Because of the Cuban missile crisis of 1962 and the United States blockade, the first wave of immigrants was terminated. The next wave would not begin until the Fall of 1965 when a special airlift program was arranged between the Cuban and United States governments. Over the next eight years, there were 260,000 Cubans airlifted to the mainland. The main purpose of the 2,800 flights was to reunite family members. The total number of Cubans who migrated to America after the revolution until 1985 was more than 800,000.

Conflict in Miami

Even though the Cuban refugees brought new vigor to Miami, there was resentment from the longtime residents. It was felt that the Cubans were receiving preferential treatment, because they had escaped a Communist dictatorship. The white, middle-class Cuban population found itself competing with the black African population for many of the same jobs. The service industry of Miami was almost completely taken over by Cubans. The Small Business Administration gave Cuban refugees forty plus million dollars in loans during the 1970's. African Americans point out that during that same period of time they received merely 6.5 million. The Cubans came to the United States better educated as a whole and also they had more business experience than most of the American minority population. The Cubans had made progress economically and wielded an ever increasing amount of political power, but they had basically done this by recreating—as closely as possible—a Cuban world for themselves. The Cuban-concentrated section of Miami can properly be considered an enclave. Cuban communities tend to remain close-knit, and in various ways support members of their communities. To an outsider, it could look like a separate country. The Cuban immigrants have, for the most part, remained close to their families as well as their native culture and not assimilated into American life.

The Language Question

Besides their culture, the Cubans also brought the Spanish language. The impact of Spanish was so great that by the 1980's Miami was definitely a bilingual city. All public notices and documents had to be printed in both Spanish and English. The issue of language flared up when a good percentage of Anglos did not approve of another language having equal status with English. There was even a campaign instigated for the purpose of having English declared Miami's "official" language.

Spanish has been the first language of the older generation that came to the United States. Spanish is their tongue and, therefore, part of what they are. The younger generation has learned to speak English and attempted to become totally American. The older generation still looks back to the life that they had in Cuba before the revolution as the ideal and have accepted change reluctantly; the younger generation seems to have recognized that they must become Americans first and Cubans second.

In 1980, Castro allowed inmates from his prisons to travel by boat to Florida. Boatloads of Marielitos (those who traveled from

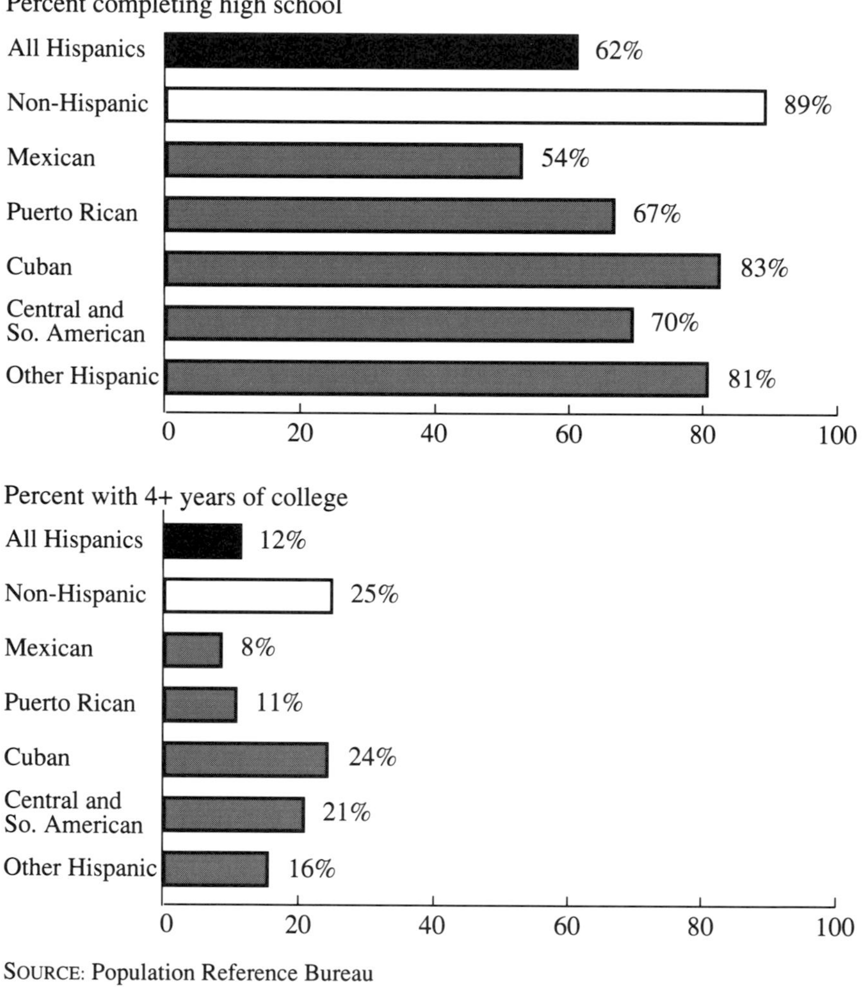
Educational Level by Hispanic Ethnic Group, 1988:
Age 25 to 34
Percent completing high school
All Hispanics
62%
Non-Hispanic
89%
Mexican
54%
Puerto Rican
67%
Cuban
83%
Central and
So. American
70%
Other Hispanic
81%
0
20
40
60
80
100
Percent with 4+ years of college
All Hispanics
12%
Non-Hispanic
25%
Mexican
8%
Puerto Rican
11%
Cuban
24%
Central and
So. American
21%
Other Hispanic
16%
0
20
40
60
80
100
SOURCE: Population Reference Bureau

the Cuban port of Mariel) arrived on the mainland to the shock and dismay of the U.S. government and members of the Cuban community. The Marielitos were not welcomed by the already-existing Cuban community. One of the reasons for this was that more than 20 percent of the Marielitos were of black Cuban descent. The majority of these new refugees merely hoped to find a job and lead a peaceful life. But there was a certain percentage that could be considered hardened criminals; the Miami police arrested sixty-six within a period of a year.

Cuban Americans are the third largest Hispanic group in the United States. The total Hispanic population, according to the 1990 Census, was more than 22 million and Cubans represent 4.9 percent of that total. Of the Hispanic subgroups, Cubans have the highest yearly median family income with $31,400. As of 1988, 83 percent of Cuban Americans between the ages of twenty-five and thirty-four had completed high school. For that same age group, 24 percent of Cubans had completed four or more years of college. Cuban Americans first came here as political refugees which makes them unique compared to most other Hispanic groups. Statistically, they are a remarkable success story. Since, for the most part, they have not ventured far outside their own communities, it is still to be decided if they will be able to assimilate into mainstream America without all the pain with which other Hispanic groups have had to deal. Their economic and political successes are probably strong indicators of how successful they will be in this endeavor.

6 The Dominican Americans

In discussions of Hispanic groups in the United States, Dominicans are often overlooked. Few people know, for example, that during the 1980's more immigrants came to New York City from the Dominican Republic than from any other country. The Population Division of the New York City Planning Commission has reported that Dominicans entered the city at the rate of 15,000 people a year—six thousand more yearly than the second largest group, immigrants from Jamaica. The number of Dominicans living in the United States had reached nearly 500,000 by the 1980's. It was not until the 1960's that the Dominican Republic began to contribute in a major way to the total number of immigrants entering the United States. The primary destination for the new immigrants was New York City—as was the case for the Puerto Ricans who came to the mainland as U.S. citizens. As it was for the Puerto Ricans, transportation was fairly inexpensive for the Dominicans coming to the mainland. The largest percentage of Dominican immigrants came to the United States looking for better incomes.

Hispaniola

The island of Hispaniola is located approximately six hundred miles southeast of Miami, Florida. The country of the

Dominican Republic makes up the eastern two-thirds of the island of Hispaniola. The other one-third of the island has become the country of Haiti. On his first voyage to the New World, Christopher Columbus reached the north coast of Hispaniola in December, 1942. The ship that Columbus had been on, the *Santa Maria*, ran aground on December 25, and the timber from the ship was used to construct a fort. The native inhabitants of the island were friendly to the Spanish and helped them build the fort. Columbus named the spot where he landed La Navidad (Christmas). He was impressed by how gentle the Tainos (the name given the native inhabitants) were and wrote that he found them to be "very openhearted people, who give what they are asked for with the best will in the world and, when asked, seem to regard themselves as having been greatly honored by the request."

Columbus was forced to leave his crew behind when he sailed back to Spain on the *Niña*. When he returned to the island in 1493, Columbus found that his crew had been killed and the fort destroyed. Columbus was still determined to establish a colony, and gave it the name of La Isabela; so the first colony in the New World was created on Hispaniola in 1493. The Spanish colonizers eventually discovered gold and silver on the island and war broke out with the Tainos over control of the land. For the next five decades, the Tainos fought to retain control of their territory, but to no avail.The Spanish settlers wiped out the entire native population. Those who were not killed in battle were victims of European diseases.

In 1496, Columbus' brother, Bartolome, founded La Nueva Isabela on the south coast of the island. This new settlement was later renamed Santo Domingo. It was located on the east bank of the Ozama River and on a safe harbor. Santo Domingo would become Spain's colonial administrative capital in the New World. The first European fortress in the Americas was built by Columbus' son, Diego, in the early 1500's. The island prospered for a number of decades until there was little gold left. The Spanish focused their attention on more promising territories like

Peru, Cuba, and Mexico. As the Spanish were losing interest in Hispaniola, adventurers from England, France, and Holland began to try their hands at becoming rich on the island. The British explorer, Sir John Hawkins, introduced African slaves to the island in 1563. The slaves were put to work on the sugar plantations that existed outside of Santo Domingo.

During the 1600's, the French established control of western Hispaniola. In 1697, with the Treaty of Ryswick, Spain turned over control of the western portion of the island to France. The French colony (now Haiti) prospered, while the Spanish section of Hispaniola declined. The Spanish finally gave up control of their portion of the island in 1795 with the Treaty of Basel. The African slaves were dissatisfied with conditions and rebelled against those who controlled them. In 1801, the Haitian leader Pierre Toussaint L'Ouverture conquered eastern Hispaniola, and in 1804 Haiti became the second independent country in the New World. Both Spain and France sent troops to regain control. In 1809, Spain took possession of their colony again, but the Haitians reclaimed it in 1822.

Dominican Independence

A successful revolt was waged against the Haitians in 1844. Juan Pablo Duarte, Ramón Mella, and Francisco del Rosario Sánchez became Dominican heroes after they led the revolt and established the Dominican Republic as an independent country. The new nation could not trust the intentions of Haiti, so they requested Spanish protection during the early 1860's. In later years, the Dominican government even asked the United States to take control of the floundering country, but opposition in the U.S. Congress prevented it from happening. Disorder finally was eliminated when Ulises Heureaux became president in 1882. The black Heureaux ruled the country like an iron-willed dictator, but the Dominican Republic saw its first prosperity under his rule. His assassination in 1899 left the country in debt to a number of

European countries. The United States, at the request of Dominican President General Carlos F. Morales, stepped in to help the Dominican Republic bring its foreign debt under control. The United States served in this capacity from 1905 to 1941.

President Woodrow Wilson sent the U.S. Marines into the Dominican Republic in 1916 in order to stop the violence that was raging between rival political factions. The military occupation brought economic progress to the nation, but also exploitation by U.S. business interests. Education and public health improved, but there was press censorship and oppressive military rule. The United States withdrew in 1924 after resentment of the occupation had grown.

The Trujillo Era

In 1930, Rafael Leónidas Trujillo Molina seized the presidency and before long he became a strong-armed dictator. He ruled the Dominican Republic for thirty years. During those thirty years, there was economic growth and political stability. Trujillo did not allow any political opposition. He modernized the cocoa, coffee, and sugar plantations, but the profits went into the pockets of the Trujillo family. Trujillo was assassinated in 1961 by member of his own army. The struggle for control of the Dominican Republic was waged by a number of factions, including the Communists, the military, the upper class, and those who wanted a democracy. The United States—once again—deemed it necessary to send in troops in 1965 after rebel forces had captured sections of Santo Domingo. Tensions eased finally in 1966 and elections could be held.

Race has not played as important a determining factor of social status in the Dominican Republic as have education, family, and economic status. A Dominican census revealed that 77 percent of the population was mulatto (mixed white and black ancestry). In the United States, mulattos were grouped together with blacks and not considered a separate group. Mulatto Dominicans found it difficult adjusting to being treated as black after they had immigrated to the mainland. As the population increased on the island, many Dominicans wished to come to the United States because there were not enough opportunities for them at home. During Trujillo's dictatorship, emigration was controlled. Trujillo's assassination and the onset of instability led to ever-increasing numbers of immigrants seeking a better life in the United States. Turmoil in the country ended after Joaquin Balaguer became president in 1966. The 1970's were very good years for the Dominican Republic. During the decade, the country could no longer be considered a planter society. The number of industrialists and professional people increased, and they became the new ruling elite. But as the population grew, industrial development could not keep pace.

Immigration to the United States

The Dominican immigrants who came to the United States in the first few decades of the twentieth century settled primarily in New York City. Since 1960, Dominicans have also settled in the manufacturing cities of the Northeast and in Miami, Florida. Since inexpensive transport was available to the Dominicans, they could move back and forth between the mainland and home without much trouble. The majority of Dominican immigrants believed that they were traveling to the United States for a temporary stay to earn money, after which they would be returning to the island. In time, however, more and more immigrants decided that they preferred living in the United States. As previous immigrant groups had done, they formed their own associations. Eventually, an ever-increasing number of Dominicans decided to fill out the naturalization papers and truly make a life for themselves in their adopted country. In New York City, they began to take an interest in local politics. The organization LUPA (Latins United for Political Action) brought Dominicans, Puerto Ricans, and other Hispanics together for a common cause.

While some Dominicans welcomed the arrival of U.S. troops in 1965, others did not; these Dominicans in New York protested against U.S. intervention and against the Communist movement in their country. (National Archives)

It has been estimated that the number of Dominicans living legally and illegally in the United States in the early 1990's had reached one million. The immigrants have worked hard to make a life for themselves in the United States. Many have had to work in semi or low-skilled jobs when they first entered the country, but strong traditional family values helped them move beyond the lower-skilled jobs. Some have opened grocery stores or small businesses while others have found white-collar occupations. Dominicans have also excelled in professional baseball since it is the national sport in the Dominican Republic. Dominican immigrants also have been eager to educate themselves and their children. Many parents have sacrificed in order to send their children to parochial schools. In comparison to some other Hispanic groups—especially the Puerto Ricans—Dominicans have made great strides in assimilating into mainstream American society.

7 The Central Americans

Before the 1960's, very few Central Americans had immigrated to the United States. The first Central Americans to be recorded as coming to the United States, arrived in 1820. The total number of Central Americans who migrated north remained under ten thousand until after 1960. These early immigrants came mainly from prosperous families of Costa Rica and Panama. The poverty and political turmoil that had motivated Hispanics from other countries to emigrate to the United States were not part of the equation for the Central Americans until comparatively late in the twentieth century. Immigration increased rapidly after some of the Central American countries became engulfed in civil wars. The number of Central Americans living in the United States by 1970 had increased to more than 150,000.

Native Americans and the Spanish Conquest

It is believed that Indians first migrated to Central America around 2000 B.C. They probably had arrived in North America more than ten thousand years ago after crossing on foot from Siberia to Alaska on a strip of land that does not exist anymore. The most famous of the Central American societies to be established was the Maya. The Mayan empire existed in northern

Central America; between A.D. 300 and 900 they were the preeminent civilization of the region. The Indian population was in a world of their own making until the Spanish conquistadors arrived in the early 1500's. Central America was swallowed up into the Spanish empire as was the West Indies, Mexico, and South America. In 1521, Gil González Dávila invaded the western portion of Nicaragua. Three years later, explorer Pedro de Alvarado and his soldiers fought for control of Guatemala. The Spanish invaders treated the Indians of Central America no better than the native peoples that they had encountered in other areas of the New World.

The Indians put up a valiant fight against the conquistadors, but they were ultimately no match for the Spanish weapons.

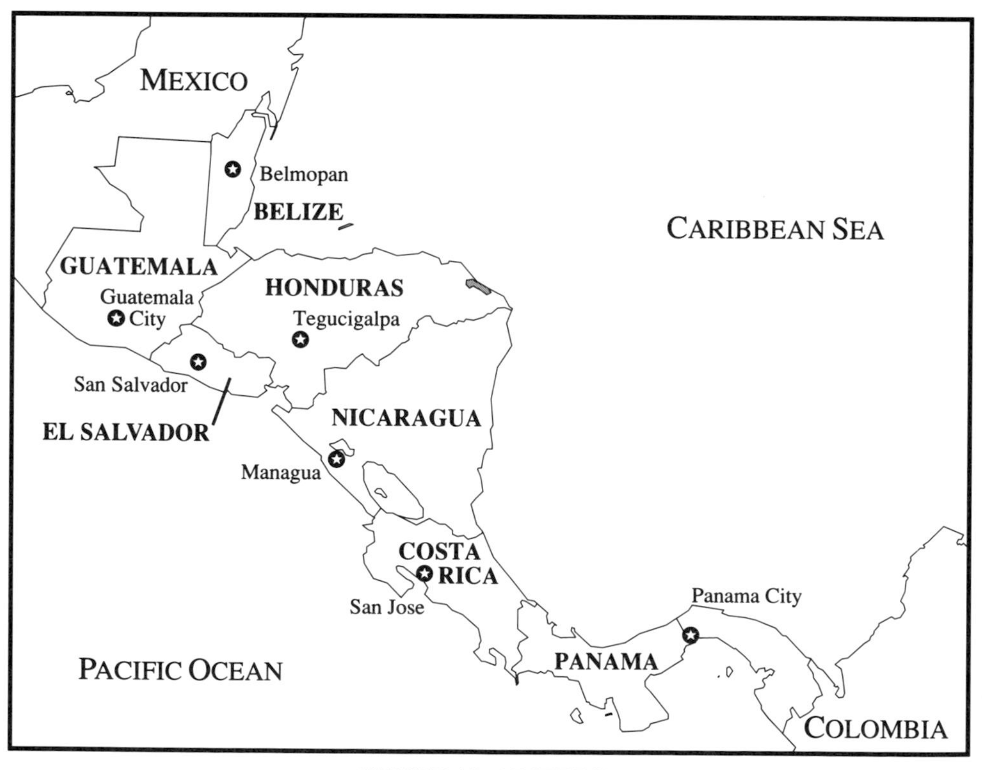

CENTRAL AMERICA

Many Indians were killed; an even larger number succumbed to European diseases to which they had no immunity. The Indians who survived became slaves of the Spanish. This brutal conquest greatly reduced the Indian population in Central America, especially in Guatemala and El Salvador. The Spanish established large ranches—known as haciendas—to grow profitable crops. In addition to laboring for their Spanish masters, the Indians also had to contend with the missionaries who were sent to convert them to Roman Catholicism. The Spanish were out to destroy every aspect of Indian life; the Indians were threatened with death if they did not adopt the Spanish religion, language, and customs as their own. Spain's stranglehold on Central America lasted until the nineteenth century.

By that time, the once mighty Spain could no longer be considered a world power. Mexico declared its independence in 1821; months later, Central America also became part of the new Mexican empire under the control of Agustín de Iturbide. His iron rule led to his downfall in 1823. A number of leading citizens met in Guatemala City and established the United Provinces of Central America, consisting of Costa Rica, Nicaragua, El Salvador, Guatemala, and Honduras. Disagreements between the five republics broke into violence, however, and the newly formed association soon collapsed. With the end of Spanish rule in the region, a void was left for another world power to fill. The British were the first to step into the breach and invest heavily in Central America. The United States wished to have European powers out of North America, and President James Monroe stated this in 1823 in what has become known as the Monroe Doctrine. But it was not until after the Mexican War in 1848 that the United States actively sought to exert influence in Central America.

American Interest in Central America

The United States began investing in various ventures in the mid-1800's. American businesses were encouraged by the U.S.

Voluntary repatriation camp for Salvadorean refugees in Honduras, 1990. (United Nations)

government to establish control of Central American commodities. It became necessary, on occasion, to send military forces into the region to protect United States investments. President William Taft used the Marines to quell unrest in Nicaragua in 1912. This established a pattern of U.S. interference in Nicaragua's internal affairs. Indeed, intervention into Central American affairs became an all too common practice for the United States. The United States government even went so far as to use its influence to prop up repressive dictatorships in Central American countries. A prime example of this is how the United States helped the Somoza family establish itself as a dynasty in Nicaragua. The Somozas controlled Nicaragua from 1936 until 1979, when the revolutionary movement known as the Sandinistas overthrew Anastasio Somoza, Jr.

Political Violence: Motive for Immigration

Political turmoil has prevailed in most of the Central American countries during the twentieth century. Thousands of people have been killed in the cross fire between repressive (usually right-wing) governments and guerrilla forces (usually left-wing). Human rights organizations have documented the activities of military death squads, bands of soldiers who employ murder and torture in an effort to terrorize the people into submission. Guerrilla forces have also been guilty of brutality and bloodshed.

Because of the violence that so many Central Americans have had to live with every day, it is not surprising that many of them have decided to flee for their lives and immigrate to the United States. The lives of Central American peasants have been so disrupted that they cannot earn a livelihood. The number of homeless in El Salvador and Guatemala has reached the hundreds of thousands. Because of the terror perpetrated by both the political left and political right, large numbers of Salvadoreans have migrated to the United States—some legally, many illegally. It has been estimated that 500,000 Salvadoreans had settled in the United States by the mid-1980's, with an estimated 300,000 in Los Angeles alone.

In general, Central Americans have tended to gravitate to the western states, although a goodly number of Panamanians and Hondurans settled in New York City. As a rule, Central American immigrants have preferred to settle in cities as opposed to rural areas because of their general educational level and the job skills which they possess. Los Angeles, New York, San Francisco, Chicago, and Miami have become the cities of choice.

Because of U.S. immigration law, it is difficult for all the Central Americans who want to come to the United States to get visas for that purpose. Thousands of Central Americans who have been displaced from their homes, because of the violence in their countries, have ended up in refugee camps in neighboring countries. The majority of Central Americans who wish to immigrate to the United States must pass through Mexico. The journey across Mexico is fraught with many dangers for the refugees. Before they have found a way to cross into the United States, refugees have become so worn down that they become easy targets for unscrupulous smugglers, who promise to get them into the United States.

The Sanctuary Movement

In the 1980's, a sanctuary movement was started as an alternative way for Central Americans to cross the border into the United States. The movement was established by hundreds of church congregations, who felt that it was the proper thing to do to break United States law, and help the Central Americans escape from the poverty and violence that they had known. Because it had been so difficult for Central Americans to prove to the U.S. government that they were fleeing their homes for fear of political persecution, the sanctuary movement has been looked upon by the refugees as a godsend. Churches have taken in the refugees and cared for them until some other arrangements could be made.

Central Americans in Los Angeles

Because of the large number of refugees from El Salvador who have migrated to Los Angeles, Los Angeles has the largest Salvadorean population outside of El Salvador. Guatemalans and Hondurans have also settled in Los Angeles in ever-growing numbers. The living conditions have not been very good for the Central Americans. In many ways, life in the city has not been an improvement over what it was like for them in the refugee camps. The Central Americans have had to work extremely hard to made a decent life for themselves. Many service organizations have been established in the United States in order to make the transition from one culture to another somewhat easier for the new immigrants. These organizations will help with food and clothing, housing, and employment advice. The Central American Refugee Center was founded to help the refugees in every way possible. This group is the largest of its kind in the United States. The majority of the Central American immigrants work as laborers; but there have been some who have started

Many Central Americans find employment as day laborers, often working for less than minimum wage. (Spencer Grant/Photobank)

their own small businesses. Education is the key to making a better life in their adopted country. The Kanjobal Indians from Guatemala have had a very hard time adjusting to life in Los Angeles, since they only speak an Indian dialect. They have tended to live in close proximity of one another, in order to support one another's efforts to survive in a completely foreign environment.

Hardships and Discrimination

Most of the Central American immigrants learn about job opportunities from relatives, friends, community groups, or churches. Men often end up in day jobs and women in domestic service. If they are undocumented refugees (without official governmental papers which legalize someone's stay in the country), finding full-time employment that pays a decent wage is almost impossible. The 1986 Immigration Control and Reform

Ontario, California; many Central American refugees and immigrants have settled in Southern California. (David Fowler)

Act made it difficult for the undocumented workers to find even unskilled employment. As long as "undocumented" carries the stigma it does in the United States, it will remain difficult for even the educated refugees to find good jobs. Being separated from their own countries has made many Central Americans feel homesick. Their image of what it would be like living in the United States had to be adjusted by the harsh realities they encountered. Central American parents, even if they cannot find a job suited to their skills, have enrolled their children in American schools. In 1982, the U.S. Supreme Court ruled in *Phyler vs. Doe* that all immigrant children were entitled to free public education, regardless of their parents' legal status. The children encountered prejudice in American public schools. Many Central American children had not gone to school in their native countries. Unfamiliarity with the educational system and not being fluent in English made the struggle doubly difficult for the immigrant children.

Even with all the hardships that Central American immigrants have had to endure, they have managed to construct communities within the United States and have made positive contributions to their adopted country. Studies have shown that the undocumented workers have added more to the economy than they have taken. Billions of dollars have been added to all levels of taxes by the Central Americans. There have been fears raised by other minority groups that the Central Americans will take jobs away from them. While in some cases this has been proven true, Central American immigrants have also generated new jobs by opening small businesses. As of March, 1991—according to the Bureau of the Census—13.8 percent of the total Hispanic population are from Central and South America. The total Hispanic population in the United States is more than 22 million, and it is the fastest growing minority in the country. Many Central Americans hope that someday they will be able to return to their native countries. Since the downfall of the Marxist Sandinista regime in Nicaragua, conditions have become more advantageous for the Nicaraguan refugees to return home. But the violent struggle has not ended in a number of other Central American countries, and so in the meantime the immigrants must make a life for themselves in the United States. For those who have prospered or have been born here, the idea of relocating back to Central American becomes more and more a remote proposition.

8 The South Americans

South America is made up of many countries, each with its own set of conditions. The immigrants who have come to the United States from South America are a diverse group, including Japanese Brazilians, middle-class blacks from Colombia, and Jewish Chileans. The majority of South American immigrants are either of Indian descent, European descent, black American descent, or some mixture of these groups. Compared to immigration from many other regions, immigration to the United States from South America has been relatively small. During the period of heaviest immigration to the United States, South America itself experienced significant immigration from Europe and, to a lesser extent, Asia. Nevertheless, political and economic instabilities within the individual South American countries have prompted some of their citizens to seek a better and hopefully more stable life in the United States. The educational level of South American immigrants tends to be higher than it is for the majority of other Hispanic groups.

Colonial South America

Europeans discovered the South American continent in 1498. The South American continent is almost twice the size of the United States. South America is currently made up of twelve

SOUTH AMERICA

countries and the province of French Guiana. Wilderness covers nearly half of the continent. There are tropical rain forests in Bolivia and Brazil, the Atacama Desert in Chile, the plains of Paraguay and Argentina, and the Andes mountain range, which runs for four thousand miles along western South America from Venezuela to Tierra del Fuego.

In Brazil, the largest country in South America, the official language is not Spanish but Portuguese. Portuguese and Spanish expeditions encountered a number of Indian tribes when they first explored the continent. The Incas had established an advanced civilization by the 1500's. They controlled a large area of South America, but they were no match for the Spanish conquistadors. Francisco Pizarro led his army into what is now Peru and, soon after, defeated the Incas and destroyed their empire. Europeans came to South America to exploit its resources. The native populations were either killed or enslaved by their conquerors. Some Europeans came in search of gold, while others established plantations to grow tobacco or sugarcane, which would then be shipped to Europe. Smallpox ravaged the native Indians, since they had no immunity to the deadly disease. During the latter part of the sixteenth century, African slaves were brought in to replace the Indians, because so many of them had died.

Independence Movements

South America remained under colonial control for more than three hundred years. The fight for independence broke out in the nineteenth century. Many of the individuals who had profited from settling in South America were resentful that they did not have more influence over their own affairs, and had to look to a European power for governmental decisions. General Simón Bolívar and his armies were able to liberate the area which makes up present-day Peru, Colombia, Bolivia, Ecuador, and Venezuela. General José de San Martín led his forces into present-day Argentina, Peru, and Chile, and was able to win independence for the area. San Martín and Bolívar combined their armies to defeat what was left of the Spanish forces. South American independence became a reality in 1824 after the Spanish army at Ayacuho, Peru, was crushed. Brazil had already won its independence from Portugal in 1822 without having to fight a revolution. Independence did not bring peace to the continent. Countless border disputes broke out and a number of wars were fought in order to settle these disputes. Some of these border disputes still have not been satisfactorily settled in the view of some of the participants.

Immigration to the United States

Even though South Americans have been migrating to the United States since the nineteenth century, the numbers did not become statistically substantial until the late 1940's. Political instability in South America led many middle-class citizens to decide that life held more promise if they immigrated to the United States. With commercial planes flying to and from South America in ever-increasing numbers, middle-class South Americans could leave their homeland more easily. The number of South Americans living in the United States by 1970 had reached more than 300,000. The total number of South American immigrants increased to approximately a half a million by 1980. The majority of immigrants settled in and around New York City, although there were some who established communities in Chicago, San Francisco, and Los Angeles. The largest number of immigrants have come from Colombia, Ecuador, and Argentina. In one particular South American country, it could be political oppression that has led its citizenry to flee; whereas, in another South American country, it could be a failed economy that drives its citizens north.

Jackson Heights, which is located in the borough of Queens in New York City, has the largest South American community in the United States. Colombians began settling there after World

War I. These Colombians who settled in Jackson Heights were highly educated and appreciated the housing and schools that they found there. Besides Colombians, South Americans from Argentina and Ecuador also have established communities within the area. The various ethnic groups have chosen to live in separate neighborhoods. Colombians tend to socialize with other Colombians, even though they may work with other Hispanics from South America on a daily basis.

The experience of Brazilians coming to the United States has been unique, since Portuguese is their native tongue. The one aspect that the South American immigrants have in common is that for the most part they are well educated. A number of Brazilians came to the United States as students and decided to stay for the time being. During the late 1980's, Brazilians began settling in ever-increasing numbers in Los Angeles, Miami, Boston, Newark, and New York City. Unfortunately, their level of education has not always led to a commensurate job. Because they speak Portuguese and not Spanish or English, they have had

Family life and family ties are of central importance in the Hispanic community. (Tony Freeman/PhotoEdit)

to overcome a greater language barrier than other South Americans.

South American immigrants have had to accept that they would not be able to instantly find a job equal to their skill level. Still, they have had an easier transition period than many other Hispanic groups. At the same time, many South American immigrants are not sure if they really want to become full-fledged citizens of the United States. They have expressed concern that North American society is too materialistic for their taste. South Americans may have physically left their homeland, but emotionally and psychologically many have remained there. In Jackson Heights, it is possible to buy many Colombian newspapers. The Catholic Church has served to help them hold onto their culture. Their children — as a rule — attend parochial schools. They have also established a number of associations in the attempt to stay close to their cultural roots.

In Chicago, a Colombian community has established itself. The Colombians of Chicago are *costeños*, which means that they have dark skin and are of mixed racial background. In Colombia, they were not the equal of the Colombians of European descent, but in the United States they frown on associating with African Americans or Puerto Ricans. South Americans in the United States have tended to construct their own distinct communities in order to retain their ethnic identity.

South Americans in the United States

Poverty has not been a major motivating factor for South Americans moving to the United States. They wanted a better life for themselves and their children, and they had the means to transport themselves to North America. In the future, there may be those who have lived in poverty, who may risk the long journey north, because conditions at home have become completely intolerable. The middle-class South Americans who have come north have made solid contributions to United States society. They have excelled in the performing arts, sciences, medicine, business, and many other fields. Since South Americans are a relatively recent immigrant group, it may take some time before they fully become active in every aspect of life in the United States. Coming here with an above-average education and technical skills gives the South Americans a head start to that end. For statistical purposes, Central and South Americans have been grouped together. According to the Population Reference Bureau, as of 1988, 70 percent of Central and South Americans between the ages of twenty-five and thirty-four had completed their high school education. In that same age range, 21 percent had completed four or more years of college, whereas the Mexican Americans were at 8 percent and the non-Hispanics were at 25 percent. Of all the Hispanic groups, the South Americans and the Cubans have been the most successful in their adopted country, and Central and South Americans have the largest percentage of their population employed, according to the March, 1991, Bureau of Census report.

9 Some Who Made a Difference

Joan Báez

Joan Báez was born on January 9, 1941 in Staten Island, New York. She is the daughter of Albert Báez, a noted physicist, and Joan Bridge Báez. Báez showed musical talent at an early age. She learned to play the guitar when she was twelve and at Palo Alto High School she sang in the choir. In the late 1950's, the family moved to Massachusetts. Báez became interested in the folk music that she heard in the Boston coffee shops. She found herself drawn to the social content of the folk songs. Being Mexican American, Báez had been the victim of prejudice, but she became determined to fight for equality for herself and others through becoming a folk singer.

At the 1959 Newport Folk Festival, Báez made her professional folksinging debut. The audience responded to her beautiful voice and her powerful songs. Throughout the 1960's and 1970's, Báez participated in a great many civil rights events for Hispanic farm workers. She also actively supported the black Civil Rights movement. In 1965, Báez founded the Institute for the Study of Nonviolence; and in 1979, she founded Humanitas International. Báez has been able to blend her musical and social concerns into a positive force. She participated in the 1985 Live Aid concert in Philadelphia. She has committed her life to worldwide human rights issues and has done work for Amnesty International. In the 1990's, Báez has not slowed down her efforts

Joan Baez. (Joan Baez)

to better the lives of those who have been victims of discrimination and to produce melodic and poignant music.

César Chávez

César Estrada Chávez was born March 31, 1927 near Yuma, Arizona, the second child of Librado Chávez and Juana Chávez. Chavez lived on a ranch that was managed by his parents until he was ten years old. They fell on hard times and they were forcibly removed from their ranch. In hopes of finding employment, the family moved to California. They became migrant workers in the Imperial Valley, but soon they had to travel to find new jobs in other parts of California. Life for them during the 1930's was extremely hard. Migrant workers were discriminated against in California. César finally dropped out of school in the eighth grade. He became frustrated and disgusted at how he was treated by the Anglo community. When he was sixteen, he was arrested for sitting in the "whites only" section of a movie theater. This experience made a lasting impression on him.

Chávez started to fight for better conditions for migrant workers in the 1940's. He soon learned that if the migrant workers were to win equality for themselves, they would have to organize. During the 1950's, Chávez perfected his organizing skills. He worked for the Community Services Organization (CSO) until 1962 when he quit because he did not believe that the organization was doing all it could for the farm workers. Chávez founded the National Farm Workers Association (NFWA) in 1962. He led the Delano grape strike of 1965, and, with the help of the AFL-CIO, the strike proved to be successful. The NFWA finally merged with an AFL-CIO organization in 1966 and became the United Farm Workers Organizing Committee (UFWOC). The organization has grown since then, and into the 1990's Chávez has continued to fight for the rights of migrant workers.

César Chávez. (Library of Congress)

Linda Chávez

Linda Chávez was born on June 17, 1947, in Albuquerque, New Mexico. The Chávez family lived there until Linda was ten years old and then they moved to Denver, Colorado. She received a parochial grade school education. Chávez went on to study English literature at the University of Colorado in Boulder. In 1970, she was graduated and subsequently she went on to do graduate work at the University of California at Los Angeles and at the University of Maryland. After doing some teaching, Chávez decided to work, first for the National Education Association, then for the American Federation of Teachers (AFT) during the 1970's. In 1977, President Jimmy Carter appointed her to the Office of Education.

Her most important appointment came in 1983 when President Ronald Reagan named her to the Civil Rights Commission. Chávez was the first Hispanic woman on the Commission. She was chosen to run the White House Office of Public Liaison in 1985. Chávez became the highest-ranking woman in the White House. In 1986, she decided to run for the U.S. Senate from Maryland. Chávez did not win the election, but she has earned respect as a talented public official. In 1991, she published a provocative study concerning Hispanics in American society entitled *Out of the Barrio: Toward a New Politics of Hispanic Assimilation*.

Jaime Escalante

Jaime Escalante was born in Bolivia in 1931. He came to prominence in 1982 when eighteen of his calculus students of Garfield High School in East Los Angeles passed their advanced placement calculus exams. Because his Hispanic students were not expected to excel, the educational authorities questioned the results of the tests. Escalante knew that his students were quite capable of passing the advanced placement exam. Not only had he taught them calculus, but also he had instilled in them the need to have pride in their own abilities. Escalante had started teaching calculus in 1964 in La Paz, Bolivia. Political instability forced him and his family to seek a better life in the United States.

Even though he had been a teacher in Bolivia, he was not allowed to teach since he could not speak English. It was not until 1974, after he had taught himself English and gone to night school at California State University to earn a math degree, that he was able to find a teaching job at Garfield. It was not until 1979 that he offered his first calculus class at the high school; only five students enrolled. The class size has increased ever since. The movie *Stand and Deliver* (1988), starring Edward James Olmos, was based on the achievements of Escalante and his students. Escalante's teaching skills and his deep concern for his students have become national assets. Escalante has shown how the educational system can work when it is driven by both discipline and concern.

Joseph M. Montoya

Joseph M. Montoya was born on September 24, 1915, in the New Mexican village of Peña Blanca. His father was a county sheriff. In 1931, he was graduated from Bernalillo High School. Montoya then went to Regis College, which is located in Denver, Colorado. He decided that he wanted to pursue a law career, so in 1934 he entered law school at Georgetown University. Before long, Montoya felt that he could serve the people best as an elected official. He ran for the New Mexico House of Representative seat from Sandoval County. Even though he was still in his second year of law school, Montoya was elected in 1936. He did go on to complete his law degree, but politics was going to be his life. Until 1957, Montoya held one New Mexican elected office or another. At the age of forty-two, he was elected to the United States House of Representatives. He was a tough, workaholic legislator and he did his best to improve the lot of the Hispanic population. Montoya moved on to the U.S. Senate in 1964, where he would remain until 1976. He proved to be an influential senator and was a staunch advocate for aid to the poor, the elderly, and Native Americans. Montoya was defeated in the 1976 election and two years later he died from complications which resulted after cancer surgery.

Richard Rodríguez

Richard Rodríguez was born on July 31, 1944, in San Francisco, California. His parents had moved there from Mexico only a few years earlier. When he was only three years old, the Rodríguezes moved to the state capital, Sacramento. Richard was a very good student at the Catholic schools he attended. He went on to attend Stanford University, where he received a B.A. degree in English in 1967. Two years later at Columbia University, Rodríguez obtained an M.A. in philosophy. He returned to the West Coast and entered the doctoral program in English at the University of California, Berkeley. He had always done well in school, but he was becoming increasingly worried that he was losing his Mexican identity. Although he completed his dissertation, Rodríguez refused to submit it in order to receive his doctorate. He decided that he needed to work out who he was by writing his autobiography.

In 1982, *Hunger of Memory* was published. The work was showered with awards, including the California Commonwealth Club gold medal for nonfiction and the Cleveland Foundation's Anisfield-Wolf award for civil rights. In *Hunger of Memory*, Rodríguez spoke critically of affirmative action and bilingual education. He believed that no matter how painful the process was that it had been better for him to become an American and not remain an "outsider" from another culture. Rodríguez expressed his concern for immigrants who seemed to flounder between one culture and another and not truly find their way in the United States. His ideas have been considered controversial, but he has continued to voice his opinions eloquently in his writings. He has also done documentary film work on Mexican immigrants. Rodríguez has attempted to remain a positive voice for his people as they struggle to reach their full potential as citizens of the United States.

10 Time Line

1492	Christopher Columbus reaches Cuba in October; reaches the island of Hispaniola (Haiti and Dominican Republic) in December.
1493	On his second voyage, Columbus lands in Puerto Rico.
1496	The oldest city in North America, Santo Domingo, is founded on Hispaniola.
1513	Juan Ponce de León sails from Puerto Rico to the coast of Florida and becomes the first European to set foot in North America.
1519-1521	Hernán Cortés and his soldiers conquer Mexico for Spain.
1565	Admiral Pedro Menéndez de Avilés founds St. Augustine (in present-day Florida), the oldest city in the United States.
1598	The first Spanish settlers arrive in New Mexico.
1610	Governor Pedro de Peralta founds Santa Fe, the second oldest city in the United States.
1776	The first college Spanish grammar and literature course in the United States is offered at the College of Philadelphia.
1821	Mexico gains its independence from Spain.
1830	Mexican migration into Texas is encouraged with the passage of the Colonization Law.
1836	Texas wins its independence from Mexico.
1848	After the defeat of Mexico in the Mexican War, the United States takes control of a large amount of territory through the Treaty of Guadalupe Hidalgo.

1849	The discovery of gold in California leads to a large influx of Anglos into the area.
1862	On May 5, Mexican rebels defeat French troops; this victory is celebrated on the holiday Cinco de Mayo.
1882	The Chinese Exclusion Act makes it possible for Mexican workers to fill jobs that had been held by Chinese.
1883	The first Latin American history course is taught in the United States at Columbia University.
1894	The Hispanic-American Alliance is founded.
1898	After the Spanish-American War, Puerto Rico is annexed by the United States and Cuba becomes independent.
1904	The Hispanic Society of America is founded.
1915	The American Association of Teachers of Spanish and Portuguese (AATSP) is founded.
1917	The Jones Act is signed by President Woodrow Wilson, giving Puerto Ricans U.S. citizenship.
1917	The United States passes an adult literacy law to restrict the number of immigrants trying to enter the country.
1919	Sociedad Nacional Hispánica Sigma Delta Pi is founded at the University of California at Berkeley (it becomes a National Society in 1925).
1924	The Immigration Act sets immigration quotas by country.
1924	The United States establishes the Border Patrol in an attempt to stop unlawful entry into the country.
1928	Mexican laborers initiate a historic strike against California's Imperial Valley melon farmers.
1929	The Hispanic Civic organization, the League of United Latin American Citizens (LULAC), is formed.
1933	The Confederation of Mexican Farm Workers' and Laborers' Unions is created.
1942	Mexico and the United States agree that Mexico will supply contract workers known as *braceros* to the United States.

1943	Anti-Mexican feelings lead to the Los Angeles Zoot Suit Riots (named because of the fashion worn by young Mexican Americans).
1946	*Méndez v. Westminster School District* outlawed separate Mexican American schools in California.
1949	Governor of Puerto Rico, Luis Muñoz Marín, establishes the Office of the Commonwealth of Puerto Rico, Dept. of Labor, Migration Division in New York in order to provide help for Puerto Ricans settling in the United States.
1952	Puerto Rico becomes a commonwealth of the United States.
1954	The United States discourages the unlawful flow of migrants through a program that becomes known as "Operation Wetback."
1960's	The Chicano movement comes to prominence.
1960	Large numbers of Cuban immigrants begin coming to United States after Fidel Castro takes control of Cuba in 1959.
1960	President Dwight Eisenhower creates the Cuban Refugee Emergency Center in Miami.
1961	The Association of Puerto Rican Executive Directors (ASPIRA) is founded in New York City for the purpose of encouraging Hispanics to further themselves through education.
1962	César Chávez founds the National Farm Workers Association.
1962	The Migration and Refugee Assistance Act becomes law.
1965	President Lyndon Johnson makes an agreement with the Cuban government which allows for an airlift between Cuba and the United States.
1965	The Immigration Act establishes immigration quotas for neighboring countries of the United States.
1965	The Voting Rights Act outlaws the poll tax, which had discouraged many Hispanics from registering to vote because they could not pay the tax.

1966	The Cuban Adjustment Act is passed.
1968	The Mexican American Legal Defense and Education Fund (MALDEF) is founded.
1968	The Bilingual Education Act intends to help school districts start bilingual programs.
1969	Mexican-American priests found Priests United for Religious, Educational, and Social Rights.
1969	The first Mexican-American college, Colegio Jacinto Treviño, is founded in Mission, Texas.
1969	The Cabinet Committee on Opportunities for Spanish Speaking People is established for the purpose of providing Spanish-speaking people access to public office.
1971	The first Conference of Americans of Hispanic Origin is held in Washington, D.C.
1980	The Refugee Assistance Act defines in legal terms a refugee as someone who seeks refuge in the United States because he or she is trying to escape persecution.
1980	Fidel Castro allows any Cuban who wants to leave from the port of Mariel to travel to the United States in the Mariel Boat Lift.
1986	The United States Congress passes the Immigration Reform and Control Act (IRCA), which attempts to resolve the illegal alien problem by granting amnesty to undocumented immigrants who have been in the country since 1982 and by imposing heavy fines on employers who knowingly hire undocumented workers.
1986	A referendum in California proclaims English as the official language of the state.

11 Bibliography

Discrimination

Allport, Gordon W. *The Nature of Prejudice*. Reading, Mass.: Addison-Welsey, 1958. This is considered a classic study on the causes of discrimination.

Gay, Kathryn. *Bigotry*. Hillside, N.J.: Enslow, 1989. Written with the younger reader in mind, this book clearly states the whys, hows, and whats of bigotry and discrimination.

Stewart, Gail B. *Discrimination*. New York: Crestwood House, 1989. A book for young readers that discusses what prejudice is and how it can lead to discrimination against a minority.

General Studies

Chávez, Linda. *Out of the Barrio: Toward a New Politics of Hispanic Assimilation*. New York: Basic Books, 1991. Chávez persuasively speaks to the strides that Hispanics have already made in assimilating into American life. She also makes the provocative contention that special preferences for Hispanics do more harm than good.

Fernández-Shaw, Carlos M. *The Hispanic Presence in North America from 1492 to Today*. New York: Facts On File, 1991. This detailed reference source is both a historical survey and a ready reference tool which gives a solid overview of the many contributions Hispanics have made to the United States.

Fuchs, Lawrence H. *The American Kaleidoscope: Race, Ethnicity, and the Civic Culture*. Hanover, N.H.: University Press of New England, 1990. A very thorough study which touches on the major issues that are of concern to the Hispanic population.

Gann, L. H., and Peter J. Duignan. *The Hispanics in the United States: A History*. Boulder, Colo.: Westview Press, 1986. An insightful and dynamic book that surveys the historical experiences of American Hispanics.

Garver, Susan, and Paula McGuire, *Coming to America: From Mexico, Cuba, and Puerto Rico*, New York: Delacorte, 1981. Written for the young adult audience, this particular volume of the series of immigrants in America speaks to the struggles that immigrants from these three countries have encountered in the United States. There are a number of firsthand experiences included which add poignancy to the plight of these Hispanic groups.

Meltzer, Milton. *The Hispanic Americans*. New York: Thomas Y. Crowell, 1982. Written for a younger audience, this book focuses on the three largest Hispanic groups—the Mexican Americans, the Puerto Ricans, and the Cuban Americans—and clarifies the crucial issues which confront them.

Parrillo, Vincent N. "The Hispanic Immigrants," in *Strangers to These Shores*. New York: John Wiley and Sons, 2d ed. 1985. A detailed textbook that looks at the various Hispanic groups living in the United States. The statistics are out-of-date but the issues raised in the chapter remain pertinent.

Ryan, Bryan, ed. *Hispanic Writers*. Detroit: Gale Research, 1991. A biographical and bibliographical guide to more than four hundred significant twentieth century Hispanic writers.

Thernstrom, Stephan, ed. *Harvard Encyclopedia of American Ethnic Groups*. Cambridge, Mass.: Harvard University Press, 1980. This book consists of extended articles on American ethnic groups. Although somewhat dated, it is still an invaluable source for looking at ethnic origins and the various histories of these groups.

Unterburger, Amy L., ed. *Who's Who Among Hispanic Americans 1991-92*. Detroit: Gale Research, 1991. A unique reference work which lists more than 5,000 Hispanic men and women with important biographical information on each of them.

Weyr, Thomas. *Hispanic U.S.A.: Breaking the Melting Pot*. New York: Harper & Row, 1988. The author persuasively points out how Hispanics have influenced United States culture in many distinct ways.

The Mexican Americans

Catalano, Julie. *The Mexican Americans*. New York: Chelsea House, 1988. Part of the Peoples of North America series, this book for young readers discusses the culture and history of Mexican Americans in straightforward fashion. There are plenty of photographs that enhance the volume.

Gómez-Quiñones, Juan. *Chicano Politics: Reality and Promise, 1940-1990*. Albuquerque: University of New Mexico Press, 1990. Focuses on the organizations and leaders that helped to shape the Chicano movement.

Mayberry, Jodine. *Mexicans*. New York: Franklin Watts, 1990. This book for young readers, which is part of the Recent American Immigrants series, focuses on the many reasons why Mexicans have migrated north and the impact they have had on their adopted country. Photographs add to the value of the volume.

The Puerto Ricans

Fitzpatrick, Joseph P. *Puerto Rican Americans: The Meaning of Migration to the Mainland*. Englewood Cliffs, N.J.: Prentice-Hall, 2d rev. ed., 1987. This perceptive study looks at the reasons why Puerto Ricans decide to migrate and the problems that they encounter once they settle in the United States.

Larsen, Ronald J. *The Puerto Ricans in America*. Minneapolis: Lerner Publications, rev. ed. 1989. Part of the In America Series, this volume concisely discusses Puerto Rican history and life for Puerto Ricans after they have moved to the mainland. The black-and-white photographs serve the volume well.

Lemann, Nicholas. "The Other Underclass." *The Atlantic* 268 (December, 1991): 96-110. This powerful article describes how Puerto Ricans remain the most poverty-stricken ethnic group in the United States even though they have made great strides.

The Cuban Americans

Gann, L.H., and Peter J. Duignan. "The Cubans," in *The Hispanics in the United States: A History*. Boulder, Colo.: Westview Press, 1986. A perceptive discussion of the unique success story Cubans have become in the United States as compared to other Hispanic groups.

Gernand, Renèe. *The Cuban Americans*. New York: Chelsea House, 1988. Written for a younger audience, this particular volume of the Peoples of North America series manages to be a solid introduction to Cuban history and the Cuban-American experience within the United States. The black-and-white and color photographs make a marvelous addition to the book.

Grenquist, Barbara. *Cubans*. New York: Franklin Watts, 1991. Part of the Recent American Immigrants series, this volume speaks to how Cubans came to the United States after Fidel Castro's Communist regime was established and how they adapted to life on the mainland. The photographs add to the overall value of the volume.

The Dominican Americans

Creed, Alexander. *Dominican Republic*. New York: Chelsea House, 1987. A concise survey of the people and history of the Dominican Republic. The role that the United States has played in its history is clearly discussed.

Echevarria, Vito. "Santo Domingo on the Hudson." *Hispanic* September 1991: 32. This article discusses how Dominicans have come to New York to find economic opportunities and have settled in Manhattan's Washington Heights.

Gann, L.H., and Peter J. Duignan. "Strangers from Many Lands: The Dominican Republic," in *The Hispanics in the United States: A History*. Boulder, Colo: Westview Press, 1986. A short but perceptive discussion of the Dominican exodus to the United States and how they have succeeded to a greater degree than the Puerto Rican minority.

The Central Americans

Bachelis, Faren. *The Central Americans*. New York: Chelsea House, 1990. Part of the Peoples of North America series, this concise volume describes how political unrest in a number of Central American countries has led to an ever-increasing number of refugees looking to find safety in the United States.

Day, Carol Olsen, and Edmund Day. "Refugees: Cubans, Central Americans, Haitians, and Soviets." *The New Immigrants*. New York: Franklin Watts, 1985. The chapter speaks to the dilemma over how the United States differentiates between Salvadoran immigrants coming north for economic reasons and refugees hoping to escape political oppression.

The South Americans

Cullison, Alan. *The South Americans*. New York: Chelsea House, 1991. This volume is part of the Peoples of North America series; it describes the diverse history of South American countries and delves into what they face as a group in the United States. The black-and-white and color photographs make a positive addition to the survey.

Gann, L.H., and Peter J. Duignan. "Strangers from Many Lands: Central and South Americans." in *The Hispanics in the United States: A History*. Boulder, Colo.: Westview Press, 1986. A brief discussion about the Colombians who have come to the United States and the relative success they have had economically.

Fiction

Anaya, Rudolfo A. *Bless Me, Ultima*, 1972. The novel concerns itself with a young boy named Antonio who lives in a small village in New Mexico during the 1940's. Anaya uses folkloric elements to illuminate the story and the mystic or *curandera* (healer) Ultima works as a benevolent force in the novel.

Arias, Ronald F. *The Road to Tamazuchale*, 1975. During the last few days that Fausto Tejada has to live, he imagines taking a journey to Tamazuchale, which becomes the representation of a person's final resting spot after his death.

Barrio, Raymond. *The Plum Plum Pickers*, 1969. Barrio describes how the migrant workers of Santa Clara County are exploited though the story of Manuel Gutiérrez and his family.

Hijuelos, Oscar. *Our House in the Last World*, 1983. This novel concerns itself with Cubans who try to adjust to life in the United States.

__________. *The Mambo Kings Play Songs of Love*, 1989. A Cuban bandleader in New York City reflects back on his life.

Hinojosa-Smith, Rolando. *Sketches of the Valley and Other Works*, 1990. This four-part novel deals with Mexican-American life in the fictitious Texas town of Klail City.

Mohr, Nicholasa. *Nilda*, 1973, 2d ed. 1986. This young adult novel concerns itself with a Puerto Rican girl who must come to terms with being a member of a minority as she grows into a teenager.

Sanchez, Thomas. *Zoot-Suit Murders*, 1978. This is a mystery set against a Mexican-American community of Los Angeles that is being terrorized by Anglo sailors in the early 1940's.

__________. *Mile Zero*, 1989. Sanchez describes the world of Key West, Florida during the 1980's. The novel also has a historical perspective by searching for the entire story of the area.

Villaseñor, Edmund. *Macho!*, 1973. The novel focuses on the hard life of a young migrant worker.

Yglesias, José. *The Truth About Them*, 1971. This novel tells the poignant story of a Cuban family struggling to find its way in Florida.

12 Media Materials

Films

The Ballad of Gregorio Cortez, 1983. Based on an actual event, this film tells the story of a San Antonio cowhand who is wrongly arrested for murder. Edward James Olmos stars as Gregorio Cortez.

The Milagro Beanfield War, 1988. Directed by Robert Redford, this film concerns itself with a farmer in New Mexico who fights against powerful Anglo land developers.

El Norte, 1984. Directed by Gregory Nava, this moving film tells the story of a brother and sister from Guatemala who make the dangerous journey from Central America to the United States.

Stand and Deliver, 1988. Based on the true story of Jaime Escalante, this film is a poignant portrait of a teacher who cares about his students and believes that they can succeed even when the educational system works against them.

Zoot Suit, 1981. Directed by Luis Valdez and based on his play, this film tells the story of a Mexican-American youth who struggles to find his identity during the 1940's when the Zoot Suit Riots were taking place in Los Angeles.

Educational Films

Against Wind and Tide: A Cuban Odyssey, 1981. A 55-minute video which focuses on the Cuban refugees who came to the United States during the Mariel Boat Lift.

Colombians in New Jersey, 1983. A documentary about the problems Colombians have had in adjusting to a new country.

Dominicans in New Jersey, 1983. This 30-minute documentary looks at the difficulties and history of the Dominicans who have migrated to New Jersey.

Manuel from Puerto Rico, 1971. This 14-minute video looks at a young Puerto Rican boy who must adjust to life in a large American city.

The Mexican American, 1977. This video is narrated by Richardo Montalban and concerns itself with the achievements that Mexican Americans have made.

Mexican Americans: An History Profile, 1983. This short video looks at Mexican-American history from the time of the Spanish conquerors to the early 1980's.

Mexican Americans: A Quest for Equality, 1983. This short video explores Mexican-American life in both rural and urban settings.

The New Underground Railroad, 1983. A 30-minute portrait of a group of church people in Wisconsin who help to smuggle Central American refugees into the United States.

13 Resources

Central American Refugee Center
3112 Mt. Pleasant St., N.W.
Washington, D.C. 20010
(202) 328-9799

Founded in 1981, the organization has made its primary concern the elimination of the problems encountered by undocumented Central American refugees who migrate to the United States.

Congressional Hispanic Caucus
Washington, D.C. 20515
(202) 226-3430

It is the purpose of the CHC to make life better for the Hispanic population through the legislative process. The Hispanic members of Congress have dedicated themselves to this cause as well as educating non-Hispanic congressional members to the needs of their constituency. The CHC also serves as a clearinghouse for research and statistical studies.

Cuban American National Council
300 S.W. 12th Ave., 3rd Floor
Miami, FL 33130
(305) 642-3484

Founded in 1972, the CNC focuses on identifying the needs of the Cuban population living in the United States. It assists them to locate governmental funding for various human services, such as counseling, vocational training, housing, and education.

Hispanic Policy Development Project
250 Park Ave., S.
New York, N.Y. 10003
(212) 529-9323

The HPDP concerns itself with raising awareness of the plight of the Hispanic population to the general public. The organization conducts research and sponsors seminars. The HPDP hopes that the lines of communication will open between the non-Hispanic and Hispanic communities.

League of United Latin American Citizens
900 E. Karen Ave., Suite C-215
Las Vegas, NV 89109
(702) 737-1240

This is the oldest and largest Hispanic civic organization in the United States. Founded in 1929, the LULAC sponsors a wide variety of social programs.

Mexican American Legal Defense and Educational Fund
634 S. Spring St., 11th Floor
Los Angeles, CA 90014
(213) 629-2512

Founded in 1968, MALDEF has offices in a number of major U.S. cities for the purpose of protecting Hispanic civil rights. Promising legal students are helped through its Law School Scholarship Program.

National Alliance of Spanish-Speaking People for Equality
1701 16th St., N.W., Suite 601
Washington, D.C. 20009
(202) 234-8198

The NASSPE is made up of Hispanic journalists and mass media workers in the United States. The organization attempts to make public the views of the Hispanic community. One of the ways that the NASSPE disseminates information is through lectures.

National Congress for Puerto Rican Rights
160 W. Lippencott St.
Philadelphia, PA 19133
(215) 634-4443

The NCPRR seeks to win civil rights for all Puerto Ricans living in the United States. Founded in 1981, it monitors legislation and gathers support for demonstrations.

Special Collections

Library of Congress
Hispanic Division
Thomas Jefferson Building, Room 204
101 Independence Ave., S.E.
Washington, D.C. 20540
(202) 287-5400

The collection contains 21 million volumes that are devoted to Spanish-American and Caribbean studies.

University of California, Los Angeles
Chicano Studies Research Library
1112 Campbell Hall
405 Hilgard Ave.
Los Angeles, CA 90024-1544
(213) 206-6052

With more than ten thousand books and other materials, the collection specializes in the experiences of Mexican Americans.

University of Texas, Austin
Benson Latin American Collection
General Libraries, SRH 1.108
Austin, TX 78713-7330
(512) 471-9241

The collection covers the history of Hispanics in the United States, as well as Mexican and Latin American social sciences and humanities. The total collection consists of more than 500,000 books and other materials.

DISCRIMINATION

HISPANIC AMERICANS STRUGGLE FOR EQUALITY

INDEX

AFL-CIO, 76
African Americans, 4, 8, 20, 24, 28, 32, 40, 46, 52, 69, 72
AFT. *See* American Federation of Teachers.
AIDS, 4
American Association of Teachers of Spanish and Portuguese, 83
American Federation of Teachers, 78
American G.I. Forum, 11, 27
Amnesty International, 74
Antonovsky, Aaron, 2
Apartheid, 4
Arawak Indians, 31, 32, 40
Argentina, 69-71
Arizona, 10, 17, 20, 22, 76
ASPIRA. *See* Association of Puerto Rican Executive Directors.
Association of Puerto Rican Executive Directors, 38, 84
Aztecs, 17

Báez, Albert, 74
Báez, Joan, 74
Balaguer, Joaquin, 54
Barrios, 26, 36, 37, 78, 86
Batista, Fulgencio, 42
Battle of Dos Ríos, 41
Battle of the Alamo, 21
Bay of Pigs invasion, 46
Bilingual Education Act, 29, 39, 85
Bless Me, Ultima (Anaya), 90
Bolívar, General Simón, 69
Bolivia, 69, 78, 79
Border Patrol, U.S., 11, 83
Boriquén, 31
Braceros, 11, 25, 83
Brazil, 67, 69-71
Bureau of Immigration, U.S., 11

Cabinet Committee on Opportunities for Spanish Speaking People, 85
California, 10, 20, 22, 26, 45, 76, 80, 83, 85. *See also* Los Angeles, California.
Caribs, 31
Carter, Jimmy, 78
Castro, Fidel, 13, 14, 42, 45, 46, 49, 84, 85
Catholic Church. *See* Roman Catholicism.
Central America, 8, 57-61. *See also* Costa Rica, El Salvador, Guatemala, Honduras, Nicaragua, *and* Panama.
Central American Refugee Center, 62, 94
Central Americans, 14, 57-66, 73, 90, 93
Chávez, César, 28, 76, 84

Chávez, Linda, 78, 86
CHC. *See* Congressional Hispanic Caucus.
Chicago, Illinois, 24, 36, 61, 70, 72
Chicano, 28, 29, 84, 88
Chicano Studies programs, 28
Chile, 67, 69
Chinese Americans, 24
Chinese Exclusion Act, 83
Christianity, 5
Civil Rights Commission, 78
Civil Rights movement, 5
CNC. *See* Cuban American National Council.
Colegio Jacinto Treviño, 85
Colombia, 67, 69-72, 90, 92
Colonization Law, 82
Colorado, 10, 22, 78, 79
Columbus, Christopher, 31, 40, 51, 82
Communism, 13, 44, 46, 53
Community Services Organization, 76
Confederation of Mexican Farm Workers' and Laborers' Unions, 83
Conference of Americans of Hispanic Origin, 85
Congress of Organizations and Puerto Rican Hometowns, 38
Congressional Hispanic Caucus, 94
Conquistadors, 17, 58, 69
Cortés, Hernán, 17, 82
Costa Rica, 57, 59
Costeños, 72
Creoles. *See* Criollos.
Criollos, 19
Cuba, 8, 13, 33, 40, 45, 82-84, 87
Cuban Adjustment Act, 84
Cuban American National Council, 94
Cuban Americans, 8, 13, 14, 40, 49, 73, 84, 85, 87, 89
Cuban missile crisis, 46
Cuban Refugee Emergency Center, 45, 84

Dávila, Gil González, 58
De Avilés, Pedro Menéndez, 82
Declaration of Independence, 1
De Coronado, Francisco Vasquez, 17
De Léon, Ponce, 31, 82
De Peralta, Pedro, 82
De San Martín, General José, 69
Díaz, José, 25
Dominican Americans, 15, 50-56, 89, 92
Dominican Republic, 8, 15, 50-54, 82
Duarte, Juan Pablo, 52

Ecuador, 69-71
Education, 11, 16, 26, 29, 36, 38, 39, 45, 47, 49, 53, 56, 61, 64, 65, 67, 71-73, 78-80
Eisenhower, Dwight D., 44, 84
El Barrio, 36, 37
El Salvador, 8, 59, 61, 62
Escalante, Jaime, 78, 79, 92

Farm workers, 28, 74, 76
Florida, 9, 38, 40, 41, 82. *See also* Miami, Florida.
Foraker Act, 33
French Guiana, 69

G.I. Bill of Rights, 27
Gachupines, 19
Gangs, 26, 36
Garment industry, 36
Great Depression, 24, 34
Guantánamo Bay, 41
Guatemala, 8, 58, 59, 61, 62, 64, 92

Haiti, 15, 51, 52, 82
Hawkins, Sir John, 52
Heureaux, Ulises, 52
Hispanic Policy Development Project, 95
Hispanic Society of America, 83
Hispaniola, 31, 50, 52, 82
Honduras, 59, 61
HPDP. *See* Hispanic Policy Development Project.
Humanitas International, 74
Hunger of Memory (Rodríguez), 80

Immigration Act of 1924, 83
Immigration Act of 1965, 84
Immigration and Naturalization Service, U.S., 27
Immigration Control and Reform Act of 1986, 65-66, 85
Immigration law of 1917, 11
Incas, 69
INS. *See* Immigration and Naturalization Service, U.S.
Institute for the Study of Nonviolence, 74
Instituto de Puerto Rico, 13

Jackson Heights, New York, 70
Jamaica, 50
Jefferson, Thomas, 1, 40
Johnson, Lyndon B., 29, 84
Jones Act, 33, 83

Kanjobal Indians, 64

"Land of the Valiant One." *See* Boriquén.
Latins United for Political Action, 54
League of United Latin American Citizens, 11, 30, 83, 95
Little Havana, 14, 45
Los Angeles, California, 20, 25, 26, 61, 62, 70, 71, 78, 92
L'Ouverture, Pierre Toussaint. *See* Toussaint L'Ouverture, Pierre.
LULAC. *See* League of United Latin American Citizens.
LUPA. *See* Latins United for Political Action.

MALDEF. *See* Mexican American Legal Defense and Education Fund.
Manual laborers. *See* Braceros.
MAPA. *See* Mexican American Political Association.
Marielitos, 13, 49, 85
Marín, Luis Muñoz, 37, 84
Martí, José, 41
Mayas, 17, 57
Mella, Ramon, 52
Méndez v. Westminster School District, 84
Mestizos, 19
Mexican American Legal Defense and Education Fund, 30, 84, 95
Mexican American Political Association, 11

Mexican Americans, 8, 10, 11, 17, 30, 73, 74, 80, 81, 83, 85, 87, 88, 93
Mexican civil war, 24
Mexican Revolution, 10
Mexican War, 10, 22, 82
Mexico, 8, 9, 11, 13, 17, 23, 59, 61, 80, 82, 83, 87
Miami, Florida, 14, 45-47, 50, 54, 61, 71, 84
Middle class, 30, 45, 46, 70, 72
Migration and Refugee Assistance Act, 84
Missionaries, 19, 59
Molina, Rafael Leónidas Trujillo, 53, 54
Monroe, James, 59
Monroe Doctrine, 59
Montoya, Joseph M., 79
Morales, Carlos F., 53
Mulatto, 15, 53

National Alliance of Spanish-Speaking People for Equality, 95
National Congress for Puerto Rican Rights, 96
National Education Association, 78
National Farm Workers Association, 76, 84
National Puerto Rican Forum, 39
Native Americans, 2, 8, 19, 20, 24, 33, 51, 57, 58, 80
Naturalization, 54
NCPRR. *See* National Congress for Puerto Rican Rights.
Nevada, 10
New Mexico, 9, 10, 17, 20, 22, 78, 79, 82
New York City, 13, 15, 33, 34, 36, 38, 39, 41, 45, 50, 54, 61, 70, 71, 74, 84, 89
NFWA. *See* National Farm Workers Association.
Nicaragua, 58-60, 65
Niña, 51

Office of the Commonwealth of Puerto Rico, Department of Labor, 37, 84
Operation Wetback, 28, 84

Panama, 57, 61
Paraguay, 69
Peru, 52, 69, 70
Philippines, 33
Phyler vs. Doe, 65
Pizarro, Francisco, 69
Platt Amendment, 41
Polk, James, 22, 40
Population Reference Bureau, 73
Priests United for Religious, Educational, and Social Rights, 85
Public schools. *See* Education.
Puerto Ricans, 13, 31-39, 72, 83, 84, 87, 88, 93
Puerto Rico, 8, 13, 31-34, 37, 82-84, 87

Reagan, Ronald, 78
Refugee Assistance Act, 85
Rodríguez, Richard, 80
Roman Catholicism, 17, 20, 22, 59, 72

San Juan Bautista. *See* Puerto Rico.
Sánchez, Francisco del Rosario, 52
Sanctuary movement, the, 14, 62, 93
Sandinistas, 60

Santa Maria, 51
Santo Domingo, 51-53, 82
Slavery, 20, 21, 33, 40, 52, 59, 69
Sleepy Lagoon Defense Committee, 25
Small Business Administration, 47
Sociedad Nacional Hispánica Sigma Delta Pi, 83
Somoza, Anastasio, Jr., 60
South Africa, 2, 4
South America, 8, 67-70. *See also* Argentina, Bolivia, Brazil, Chile, Colombia, Ecuador, French Guiana, Paraguay, Peru, *and* Venezuela.
South Americans, 14, 67-73, 90, 92
Southwestern United States, 8, 10, 22, 25, 26
Spain, 5, 9, 17, 19, 20, 31-33, 40, 51, 52
Spanish-American War, 33, 41, 83
Stand and Deliver, 79, 92
Sugar, 33, 34, 40, 42, 52, 53, 69

Taft, William, 60
Tainos, 51
Ten Years' War, 41
Texan Revolution, 21
Texas, 10, 17, 20-22, 26, 82, 85
Tijerina, Reies López, 28
Tobacco, 40, 41, 69
Toussaint L'Ouverture, Pierre, 52
Treaty of Basel, 52
Treaty of Guadalupe Hidalgo, 10, 22, 82
Treaty of Paris, 33
Treaty of Ryswick, 52
Trujillo, Rafael, 15
Twenty-sixth Amendment, 6, 7

UFWOC. *See* United Farm Workers Organizing Committee.
Underclass, 88
United Farm Workers Organizing Committee, 76
United Nations, 1
U.S.S. Maine, 33, 41
Utah, 10, 22

Vaqueros, 22
Velázquez, Diego, 40
Venezuela, 69
Violence, in the United States, 25
Violence, outside the United States, 60
Voting Rights Act, 84

Wetback, 28
Wilson, Woodrow, 53, 83
World War I, 24
World War II, 5, 11, 25, 27, 36
Wyoming, 10, 22

Zoot Suit Riots, 25, 83, 92